the *Amish Way* cookbook

A WORD OF THANKS

I would like to express my thanks to all of the Amish homemakers in Ohio and Pennsylvania who made this book possible by sharing their favorite recipes. Unfortunately, some of the recipes received did not bear the name of their contributors, and could not be identified. Some of the dishes have been passed down through generations and possess the flavor of the Amish culture from which they evolved. Others are up to date and utilize modern prepared foods as part of their ingredients. Regardless of their vintage, I have found them delicious and economical and very easy to prepare.

THE ARTISTS

I wish to express my appreciation to Mr. Florian K. Lawton for the beautiful illustration on the cover. Mr. Lawton is a native Ohioan and is internationally renowned for his outstanding abilities as an artist. His love for the Amish people has given his paintings a special sensitivity and a touching glimpse into the lives of "the gentle people".

I would also like to thank Walter C. Pitts of Louisville, Ky. for his excellent illustrations throughout the book. Mr. Pitts is well known for his abilities as a teacher, graphic designer and painter. He is the recipient of many awards in his field.

THE AMISH WAY OF LIFE

The Amish arrived in America about 300 years ago and have settled in rural communities in 20 of the United States. They are direct descendants of the Anabaptists, who originated in Germany, France, Switzerland and the Netherlands. At one time, they belonged to the Old Order of Mennonites, but due to disagreements over the practice of infant baptism, the Amish, led by Jacob Ammon, broke away from the parent religion and formed their own sect.

The Amish base their lives on the teachings of the Bible. They regard the customs and belief of their forefathers very highly and cling to the same manner of worship, style of dress and traditions.

The Amish do not own automobiles, tractors, radios or television sets. They do not have electricity in their homes. They do not accept funds from the government nor do they run for office. They believe in helping each other in times of need and are a loving, gentle people. They do not believe in warfare.

The Amish children attend schools which have been built by the Amish. The schools provide formal education up to the eighth grade. The boys are trained to be skilled farmers, carpenters, masons and blacksmiths. The girls are taught to cook and sew at an early age.

The Amish women are famous for their delicious cooking and baking. Their recipes are widely sought and enjoyed by many as they are usually prepared with simple, nourishing ingredients that are easy to find and are part of our everyday staples.

The style of dress is neat. The women and girls wear dresses in solid colors and use straight pins to fasten them, instead of buttons. They do not cut their hair and wear it pinned up in the back with a small white "Kapp" covering it. The men wear plain, dark pants. They also wear a special dark colored split tailed coat when attending church. When men join church or get married they must wear a beard.

The Amish people live to serve God and their fellow man in love kindness and humility and have separated themselves from worldliness in order to attain as close a relationship with God as possible.

Breads and Rolls

MOTHER'S RECIPES

Some women have a pantry filled,
with spices, herbs and stuff,
salt and pepper, yeast and flour,
but that's not quite enough.

My Mom's the finest cook around,
and she told me long ago,
that bread's no good unless you add
some lovin' to the dough.

An when you're baking pies,
says she, a pinch of faith and trust,
if added to the shortening,
makes a tender, flaky crust.

You must add a cup of patience,
when making cookie dough,
with temperance as your partner,
place them in a neat row.

Add some kindness to your yeast
and when the doughnuts rise,
they'll sweeter be, (though made in grease),
you'll meet a glad surprise.

And compassion by the spoonful
when added to a cake,
makes it come out light and fluffy.
Just the finest you can make.

Now these things can't be purchased
in the store across the way,
but Mother keeps them in her heart
and uses them each day.

Mrs. Jonas V. Miller

4

SUNNY CORN MUFFINS

1/2 c. butter
1/2 c. brown sugar
1 egg
1 c. milk
1 tsp. salt

1 tsp. soda
2 tsp. cream of tartar
1 c. corn meal
1 c. flour

Preheat oven to 375°. Cream sugar and butter. Add remainder of ingredients. Mix well. Fill greased muffin pan cups a little more than ½ full. Bake at 375° for 20-25 minutes.

CORN PONE

2/3 c. sugar
3/4 c. corn meal
1 c. flour
2 tsp. baking powder

pinch of salt
1 egg
1/2 c. milk
1/2 c. cooking oil

Preheat oven to 350°. Mix all ingredients, stirring oil in last. Beat well and bake in a greased pan at 350° until done.

Mrs. William J. Hochstetler

PUMPKIN BREAD

1-1/2 c. plus 2 tbsp. flour
1-1/2 c. sugar
3/4 tsp. salt
1 tsp. soda
1/2 tsp. cinnamon

1/2 tsp. nutmeg
1/2 c. melted shortening
2 eggs, beaten
1/3 c. water
1 c. canned pumpkin

Preheat oven to 350°. Sift dry ingredients into large mixing bowl. In another bowl beat together the rest of the ingredients. Mix only until dry ingredients are moist. Bake in greased and floured 9x5x3 pan in 350° oven for 60 to 65 minutes.

Mrs. Allen Mullet

COFFEE CAKE

1 c. milk
1 stick butter
1/2 c. sugar
1 tsp. salt

2 eggs
1 pkg. yeast
1/4 c. warm water
3-1/2 c. flour

Preheat oven to 325°. Scald milk and add butter. Cool. Add sugar and salt to milk mixture. Beat eggs and add. Dissolve yeast in warm water and add to mixture. Mix in flour. Cover and let rise overnight. In the morning, put in three greased pie pans and spread with crumb mixture. Let rise again. Bake at 325° for 15 minutes. Cool, split and fill.

Crumbs:
1/2 c. brown sugar
1/2 c. flour

1/4 c. butter

Mix well and spread on top.

Filling:
1 egg white, beaten
2-1/4 c. confectioner's
  sugar
pinch of salt

3 tbsp. water
1/4 c. white sugar
1/2 c. Crisco
1 tsp. vanilla

Beat egg white and add sugar and salt. Boil 3 tbsp. water with 1/4 c. sugar for 3 minutes. Pour into egg white mixture. Stir in 1/2 c. Crisco and 1 tsp. vanilla.

Mrs. Crist J. Miller

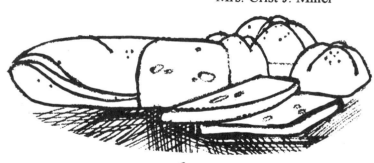

FASTNACHTS

1-1/2 c. milk
1/4 c. light molasses
1 tsp. salt
1/4 c. soft butter
1 pkg. active dry yeast
1/4 c. warm water
  (105-115°)

1 egg, beaten
4-1/4 to 4-1/2 c. sifted
  all-purpose flour
salad oil or shortening
granulated sugar

Heat milk in medium saucepan just until bubbles form around edge of pan. Add molasses, salt and butter, stirring until butter is melted. Remove from heat and let cool to lukewarm. In large bowl of electric mixer, sprinkle yeast over warm water, stir until dissolved. Add milk mixture, egg and 2 c. flour, beating until smooth. Dough will be soft. Cover with damp towel. Let rise in warm place (85°) free from drafts, until double in bulk, about one hour. Punch dough down. If dough seems too soft to handle, work in additional 1/4 c. flour.

Turn out dough onto well-floured pastry cloth, rolling over to coat lightly with flour. Knead 10 times to make a smooth dough. Cover with mixing bowl; let dough rest 10 minutes. Divide dough in half. Roll out 1/2 inch thick. Cut with floured 3-inch doughnut cutter. Press remaining dough into a ball. Reroll and cut. With wide spatula, transfer cut doughnuts to top edge of pastry cloth. Cover with towel; let rise until double in bulk, 30-40 minutes. Meanwhile, in electric skillet or heavy saucepan, slowly heat salad oil (1-1/2 to 2 inches deep) to 375° on deep-frying thermometer. Gently drop doughnuts, 3 to 4 at a time, and "holes" into hot oil. As they rise to surface, turn over with slotted utensil. Fry until golden brown on both sides; about 3 minutes in all. With slotted utensil, lift doughnuts from oil; hold over skillet a few seconds to drain slightly. Drain well on paper towels. Roll in sugar. Makes about 2 dozen.

Mrs. Eileen Miller

REFRIGERATOR ROLLS

2 pkg. yeast
2 c. water
1/2 c. sugar
2 tsp. salt

6-1/2 to 7 c. all-purpose
   flour (sifted)
1 egg
1/4 c. Wesson oil

Soften yeast in lukewarm water. Add sugar and salt and about
1/2 of flour. Beat thoroughly 2 minutes; add egg and Wesson
oil. Gradually beat in remaining flour until smooth. Cover with
damp cloth and wax paper. Place in refrigerator. Punch down
occasionally as dough rises in refrigerator. About 2 hours before
baking, cut off amount needed and shape into rolls. Place on
greased baking sheet, cover and let rise until light (1-1/2 to 2
hours). Heat oven to 400° and bake 12 to 15 minutes. Makes 4
dozen medium rolls. Dough can be kept in refrigerator or ice
box 3 or 4 days.

Mrs. Joseph J. Weaver

DREAM BISCUITS

1 c. flour
1/2 tsp. salt
2 tsp. sugar

2 tsp. baking powder
3 tbsp. shortening
1/2 c. milk

Preheat oven to 450°.
Cut in shortening into dry ingredients. Add milk. Roll out and
cut. Bake 10-12 minutes at 450°.

Emma Beachy

SWEDISH TEA RING

1/3 c. very warm water	1/2 c. butter, melted
1 pkg. yeast	1/2 tsp. vanilla
1/2 c. milk, scalded	2 eggs
1/2 c. sugar	

Combine yeast and warm water until dissolved. Add sugar, salt butter and milk. Combine milk mixture with dissolved yeast. Add 1-1/2 c. flour and mix well. Add eggs and vanilla. Then add enough flour to make sticky dough - not too stiff. Cover with damp cloth and let rise 1-1/2 to 2 hours. Roll out into rectangle on floured board and roll thin. Spread with soft butter and sprinkle with brown sugar and nuts. Roll up and bring end to form a ring. Place on greased cookie sheet and cut every 2 inches. Let rise 1/2 hour to 45 minutes. Bake at 350° for 20 to 30 minutes. While hot, put on icing and sprinkle with nuts.

ICING:

1-1/2 c. powdered sugar	2 tbsp. milk
2 tbsp. soft butter	1 tsp. maple flavor

CINNAMON OVERNIGHT ROLLS

1/2 c. warm water	1 c. oil
2 tbsp. sugar	2 eggs, beaten
2 pkgs. yeast	1-1/2 c. sugar
4 c. warm water	14 c. flour
3 tsp. salt	

Mix first three ingredients in bowl and let stand for 10 minutes. Mix 4 c. water, salt, oil , eggs and sugar. Add in flour gradually, beating as long as possible. Let rise for 2 hours. Punch down. (continued)

Let rise again for 2 hours. Roll out 1/2 inch thick. Dot with butter, sprinkle with cinnamon and sugar; roll jelly-roll fashion and cut into pieces. Place in greased pan. let stand overnight. Bake at 375° for 12 to 15 minutes. Frost with maple or vanilla frosting.

Mrs. Urie M. Byler

DILLY BUNS

1 pkg. yeast	1 c. small curd cottage
1/4 c. warm water	cheese
2 tbsp. sugar	1 tbsp. dill seed
1 tbsp. dry onion flakes	1/4 tsp. soda
1 tbsp. butter	1 egg
1 tsp. salt or less	2-1/2 c. flour

Dissolve yeast in water. Put all ingredients but flour in a large mixing bowl. Mix well. Add flour slowly, beating after each addition. Cover with cloth. Let rise until double; about 1 hour. Stir down and form into small buns. Place on greased pan and let rise until light - about 30 minutes. Bake in 350° oven for 12 minutes or until golden brown - 40 to 45 minutes for a loaf. Remove from pans, brush with butter and sprinkle with salt. Bakes 12 buns.

Katherine M. Byler

ORANGE NUT BREAD

rind of one orange, grated	1 egg, beaten
1/2 c. water	1 c. sifted flour
1 tsp. salt	1 c. whole wheat flour
1/2 c. sugar	2 tsp. baking powder
juice of one orange	1/2 tsp. soda
enough milk added to orange	1/4 c. shortening
juice to make one cup	1/2 c. chopped nuts

Combine orange rind, water, salt and sugar and boil for 10 minutes. Cool. Add milk to orange juice, then add cooled mixture. Sift flours with baking powder and soda. Cut in shortening until mixture is like meal. Pour liquids into dry ingredients and stir vigorously until well mixed. Add nuts and blend. Bake in loaf pan in 350° oven 50 to 60 minutes.

ZUCCHINI BREAD

3 c. flour	1 tsp. cinnamon
3 eggs	1 tsp. salt
2 c. sugar	1 tsp. soda
1 c. oil	1/4 tsp. baking powder
1 tsp. vanilla	1/2 c. sour cream
2 c. grated zucchini	1 c. nuts or raisins

Preheat oven to 350°. Mix all ingredients together. Pour into two greased loaf pans 9x5x3. Bake at 350° for one hour.

BANANA NUT BREAD

1/2 c. shortening	2 c. pastry flour
1 c. sugar	1 tsp. soda
2 eggs, beaten	3 ripe bananas, mashed

Preheat oven to 325°. Mix well and bake in a well greased loaf pan or small bread pans. Bake at 325° for 1 hour.

Edna D. Yoder

BLUEBERRY MUFFINS

1-3/4 c. flour
1/4 c. sugar
2-1/2 tsp. baking powder
3/4 tsp. salt
3/4 c. milk

1 egg, well beaten
1/3 c. cooking oil
1 c. blueberries
2 tbsp. sugar

Mix flour, sugar, baking powder and salt. Make a well in the center of the flour mixture. Combine milk, eggs and oil and add flour. Stir until dry ingredients are moistened. Toss in blueberries and 2 tbsp. of sugar. Stir gently into batter and pour into greased pans. Bake at 400° for about 25 minutes. While warm, dip tops into melted butter and then sugar. Makes 12 muffins.

Mrs. Jake A. Byler

CHOCOLATE CHIP SOUR CREAM COFFEE CAKE

3 c. flour
3 tsp. baking powder
1 tsp. baking soda
1 tsp. salt
1 c. sugar
1 c. sour cream

3 eggs
1 tsp. cinnamon
1 c. butter
1 tsp. vanilla
1 pkg. chocolate chips
1/2 c. brown sugar, packed

Combine, flour, baking powder, soda and salt. Cream together butter and white sugar. Add eggs one at a time, beating thoroughly after each addition. Add vanilla. Add dry ingredients alternately with sour cream to creamed mixture, ending with dry ingredients. Combine chocolate chips, brown sugar and cinnamon. Spoon half of the batter into a greased 13x9x2 cake pan. Sprinkle with 3/4 of chocolate mixture and cover with rest of batter, and sprinkle with remaining chocolate mixture. Bake in 350° oven about 30-35 minutes.

PANCAKES

1 c. flour	1 tsp. soda
1 egg	1 tbsp. lard
2 tbsp. sugar	1/4 tsp. baking powder
	sour milk, as needed

*Shortening may be used instead of lard.

Mix all ingredients together. Add enough sour milk to make batter as thin as you wish. Fry in hot, oiled skillet.

Betty Shrock

COLORS FOR MARRIAGE

Marry in red, you'll wish yourself dead.

Marry in black, you'll wish yourself back.

Marry in brown, you'll live in town.

Marry in yeller, you'll be shamed of your feller.

Marry in green, you'll be ashamed to be seen.

Marry in blue, you'll always be true.

Marry in white, you'll always do right.

Mrs. Robert Gingerich

CREAM FILLED DOUGHNUTS

2 pkg. yeast
1 tsp. sugar
1 c. warm water
1 c. scalded milk
2/3 c. sugar

1/2 c. butter, melted
1/2 c. lard
1-1/2 tsp. salt
6-1/2 c. flour
2 eggs, beaten

*shortening may be used instead of lard.

Mix yeast, sugar and warm water. Let stand for five minutes.
Add beaten eggs, butter, shortening and milk to yeast mixture.
Mix dry ingredients together and add gradually to rest. Place in
a bowl and let rise until double in size. Roll to 1/2 inch thick.
Cut doughnuts with round cutter or glass dipped in flour and let
rise again about 30 minutes. Fry in deep fat (370°). Drain on
absorbent paper. Punch hole in side of doughnut while hot.

Filling:

4 egg whites
3/4 c. Crisco
1-1/2 c. powdered sugar

1 jar marshmallow cream
1 tsp. vanilla

Beat until light and fluffy. Put inside doughnut through hole or
slice doughnut and spoon in.

Mrs. Crist Miller

CINNAMON ROLLS

1 c. lukewarm milk   1/2 c. warm water
1/2 c. sugar   2 eggs
1/2 c. shortening   1 tsp. salt
2 pkgs. yeast   4-1/2 to 5 c. flour

soft butter   brown sugar
cinnamon

Dissolve yeast in warm water. Mix flour, salt, sugar and shortening until consistency of coarse meal. Add yeast mixture and beaten eggs to milk. Combine with flour mixture and mix well. Work dough two times before doing following. Roll dough to 1/2 in. thick. Spread with soft butter and brown sugar. Sprinkle with cinnamon. Cut into one inch slices. Place in greased muffin tins or large cake pan. Let rise in warm place until double. Bake in 350° oven for 20-25 minutes. Glaze while warm with confectioner's sugar icing.

Sovilla Miller

BISCUIT MIX

8 c. flour   1/3 c. baking powder
8 tsp. sugar   2 tsp. cream of tartar
2 tsp. salt   1 c. powdered milk
1-3/4 c. shortening

Sift dry ingredients 3 times and cut in shortening. Pack in airtight container. When needed, mix 1 cup of mix with 1/3 c. water. Mix and then bake at 450° for 10-12 minutes.

Katherine M. Byler

15

CREAM STICKS

2 pkg. yeast dissolved in
   1 c. warm water
1 c. scalded milk
1/2 c. margarine
2/3 c. sugar

2 eggs
1/2 tsp. salt
1 tsp. vanilla
6 c. flour

Let dough rise until double in size. Knead and form into sticks 3-1/2 x 1-1/2 inches. Let rise again. Deep fat fry.

Filling:
3 tbsp. flour

1 c. milk

Cook flour and milk together until thickened slightly.

Cream:
1 c. sugar
1 tsp. vanilla

1 c. Crisco
2-1/2 c. powdered sugar

Add flour and milk mixture to sugar, Crisco and vanilla. Mix well. Add powdered sugar, beat until creamy. Split open top of fried cream sticks and fill. Frost with the following:

Frosting:
1/2 c. brown sugar
4 tbsp. butter

2 tbsp. milk

Mix and heat to a boil. Cool. Add powdered sugar and vanilla. When cool, spread over top of cream sticks.

SOUR CREAM COFFEE CAKE

1/2 c. butter
1 c. sugar
1 tsp. soda
2 c. flour
1 c. sour cream.

2 eggs
1 tsp. baking powder
1/2 tsp. salt
1 tsp. vanilla

Preheat oven to 325°. Cream together butter, eggs and sugar. Sift together dry ingredients and add to mixture. Add sour cream and vanilla. Pour batter into 9 in. pan that has been buttered. Power 3/4 of topping on top and swirl with fork. Sprinkle remaining on top. Bake 40 minutes in 325° oven.

Filling and topping:

1/2 c. brown sugar
1 tsp. cinnamon

1/4 c. melted butter

Mrs. Ray Byler

ANGEL BISCUITS

1 pkg. dry yeast
1/4 c. warm water
2-1/2 c. flour
1/2 tsp. baking powder
1 tsp. soda

1 tsp. salt
1/8 c. sugar
1/2 c. shortening
1 c. buttermilk

Preheat oven to 400°. Dissolve yeast in warm water. Mix dry ingredients, cutting in shortening as for biscuits. Stir in buttermilk; also yeast and water mixture. Dough can be refrigerated. Knead lightly, roll and cut on floured board. Place on greased pan. Bake at 400° until light golden-brown.

Barbara Miller

NEVER FAIL BREAD

4 c. warm water	1/3 c. oil
2 pkg. dry yeast	2 tsp. salt
1/3 c. sugar	12 c. flour

Preheat oven to 400°. Add yeast to warm water and mix well. Add sugar, oil and salt. Add flour gradually. Let rise in warm place for 1 hour. Punch down and let rise another hour. Shape it into loaves and let rise in greased loaf pans for 1 to 1-1/2 hours. Bake at 400° for 35 minutes.

Martha M. Byler

IRISH FRECKLE BREAD

2 potatoes, cooked and mashed	1 tsp. salt
	8 tbsp. sugar
1 c. warm water	2 eggs, beaten
2 pkgs. yeast	1 c. raisins
1/2 c. margarine	5-1/4 c. flour

Mix yeast in warm water. Let stand for 5-10 minutes. Add mashed potatoes, margarine, salt, sugar, eggs and raisins. Mix well. Let rise and then punch down. Put in greased loaf pans. Let rise again. Bake at 350° until golden brown. Frost bread with confectioner's sugar frosting.

Mrs. Urie M. Byler

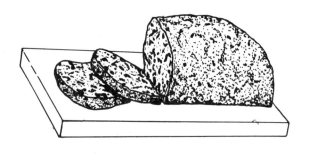

CINNAMON RAISIN BREAD

1/2 c. lukewarm water	1 c. flour - plus
2 pkgs. yeast	1/4 c. shortening
1-1/2 c. lukewarm milk	1 egg, beaten
1/4 c. sugar	1/2 c. sugar
2 tsp. salt	2 tbsp. cinnamon

Dissolve yeast in lukewarm water. Soak for five minutes. Combine lukewarm milk, 1/4 c. sugar and salt. Add 1 cup flour, shortening and beaten egg. Continue to add flour until you get a soft dough. Let rise for 1 hour. Punch down and let rise again. Mix 1/2 c. sugar and cinnamon. Roll dough into rectangle about 1/2 in. thick. Sprinkle with sugar and cinnamon mixture and roll like a jelly roll. Let rise again and bake at 350 ° for about 30 minutes.

Esther Schmucker

HOBO BREAD

1 c. raisins	2 tbsp. vegetable oil
2 tsp soda	1 c. brown sugar
1 c. boiling water	1/2 tsp. salt
2 c. flour	

Place raisins, soda and water in a covered pot and let stand overnight. Bring to a boil. When cool, add dry ingredients and oil and mix well. Add raisin mixture. Put in greased loaf pan. Bake at 350° for 1 hour. Makes 1 small loaf.

Kathryn Byler

WHITE BREAD

3 tbsp. sugar
1 tbsp. salt
2 tbsp. lard
1-1/2 c. boiling water

3/4 c. cold water
3 1/2 c. flour
2 pkg. yeast

Preheat oven to 350°. Combine first four ingredients and stir. Add cold water, flour and yeast. Stir together until smooth. Cover and let stand 15 minutes. Add flour, a little at a time until all is worked in (use more flour if not the right texture). Bake at 350° for 30-35 minutes. (shortening may be substituted for lard)

Laura V. Troyer

RAISIN BREAD

4 pkg. yeast
1 c. lukewarm water
4 c. raisins
1 c. margarine
1 c. sugar

2 tsp. salt
2 c. scalded milk, cooled
8 eggs
12 c. flour

Preheat oven to 350°. Dissolve yeast in warm water. Set aside. Mix raisins, margarine, sugar, salt and cooled, scalded milk. Add eggs and yeast mixture. Gradually add about 12 c. of flour until you get a soft dough. Let rise once. Pour into greased pans and let rise again until double in size. Bake at 350° for 35 minutes.

Sovilla Miller

CRACKED WHEAT BREAD

2 pkg. dry yeast	2 c. scalded milk
1/2 c. lukewarm water	3 tbsp. sugar
1-1/2 c. cracked wheat	2 tbsp. salt
9 c. flour	4 tbsp. lard (shortening may be
2 c. cold water	used in place of lard)

Dissolve yeast in 1/2 c. lukewarm water. Mix cold water and scalded milk. Mix dry ingredients together, mix yeast, milk mixture and shortening, and add this liquid to dry ingredients gradually, mixing in between additions.

Dough should be almost too moist to knead, but can be kneaded with greased hands. Punch down after letting it rise to double in size. Let rise again, then knead into three loaves. Place in greased loaf pans, and let rise to double. Bake in 400° oven for 25 minutes, then reduce temperature to 275° and bake for 25 minutes more.

Mrs. Harvey W. Byler

THE CRUST OF BREAD

I must not throw upon the floor,
The crust I cannot eat.
For many little hungry ones,
Would think it quite a treat.

My parents labor very hard,
To get me wholesome food,
So I must never waste a bit,
That would do others good.

For willfull waste makes woeful want,
And I might live to say,
"Oh, how I wish I had the bread,
that once I threw away."

Mrs. David Ray Yoder

WHITE BREAD

2 c. milk, scalded
2 tbsp. sugar
1 tbsp. salt
2 tbsp. lard (shortening
   may be used instead)

2 pkg. yeast
1/4 c. lukewarm water
1 tsp. sugar
6 c. Robin Hood flour

Cool scalded milk to lukewarm and then add 2 tbsp. sugar and 1 tbsp.salt. Add lard and stir until dissolved. Meanwhile, dissolve yeast in lukewarm water, adding 1 tsp. sugar. Pour both mixtures into large Tupperware type bowl. Gradually add flour. Mix until hard to stir, then knead in bowl with hands, not using all the flour. Keep the dough light, but not sticky. Cover lightly and let rise in a warm place. Punch down a little. Let rise again. Wipe sweat off of bowl cover and, using some leftover flour, spread dough on cover and divide into two parts. Knead a little and put into greased bread pans. Cover with a tea towel and let rise again for an hour or two. When light, bake in 350° oven until nicely browned - 35 to 45 minutes. Cool and brush with butter. Makes two loaves.

Mrs. William Hochstetler

ZUCCHINI MUFFINS

2 c. whole wheat flour
1 tbsp. baking powder
1 tsp. cinnamon
3/4 tsp. salt
2 eggs

3/4 c. milk
1/3 c. oil
1/4 c. honey
1 c. coarsely grated zucchini
2/3 c. raisins

Preheat oven to 375°. Oil muffin pans. Stir or sift together dry ingredients. In small bowl, beat eggs, milk, honey and oil. Add to dry ingredients, stirring just enough to moisten. Quickly stir in zucchini and raisins and spoon into greased muffin pans. Bake 20-25 minutes or until golden brown. Makes 12-15.

GLAZED DOUGHNUTS

1 cake yeast	7 c. sifted flour
1 c. warm water	1/2 c. melted shortening
1 c. milk, scalded	2 eggs
1/2 c. sugar	1 tsp. vanilla
1 tsp. salt	

Dissolve yeast in warm water. Mix milk, sugar and salt together. Cool to lukewarm. Add yeast mixture to milk. Add 4 c. flour, one cup at a time. Beat after each addition. Add melted shortening and beat in eggs, vanilla, and nutmeg. Add 3 more cups flour. Knead until smooth. Let rise until doubled in bulk; about 2-1/2 hours. Punch down and roll 1/2 in thick on floured board. Cut with doughnut cutter. Let rise about half. Fry in deep fat. Glaze while warm.

Maple Glaze:

1/2 c. maple syrup	1 tsp. vanilla
2 c. confectioner's sugar sifted	1 tbsp. hot water

Dip doughnuts in glaze.

WAFFLES

2 c. flour	1/4 tsp. salt
2 tsp. (rounded) baking powder	3 eggs
5 tbsp. butter	2 c. milk

Put flour, baking powder, sugar, salt in bowl. Add beaten egg yolks and milk. Beat well and add melted butter. Fold in stiffly-beaten egg whites and bake on waffle iron.

Mrs. Ervin E. C. Miller

PANCAKES

1 c. flour
2 tsp. baking powder
1 tbsp. sugar
1/4 tsp. salt

1 egg
1 c. milk
3 tbsp. shortening

Combine ingredients and fry in small amount of oil.

Mrs. Henry A. Miller

CINNAMON ROLLS

1-1/4 qt. lukewarm water
4 cakes yeast
1 tsp. salt
4 eggs, beaten
2 c. sugar

5 lb. flour
melted butter
cinnamon
brown sugar

Combine water, yeast, salt, eggs, white sugar and flour. Let rise until double in size. Punch down and let rise again. Roll out and brush with melted butter, cinnamon and brown sugar. Roll up and cut in 1 in. slices. Bake at 350° for approximately 20-25 minutes. Frost with powdered sugar icing and sprinkle with nuts.

CHELSEA BUNS

1 pkg. dry yeast
1/2 c. cooled mashed
    potatoes
1/3 c. melted shortening
2 well beaten eggs
(continued)

1/2 c. lukewarm water
1 tsp. sugar
1/3 c. sugar
1/2 tsp. salt
2-1/2 c. flour

Combine potato, water and 1 tsp. sugar. Sprinkle yeast on top. Let stand for fifteen minutes. Add the remaining ingredients, stirring in enough flour to make a soft dough (not as stiff as bread dough). Knead until smooth. Let rise until double in bulk.

Spread following ingredients in a greased 9x13 pan, putting the nuts in last:

2 tbsp. soft butter	1/2 tsp. vanilla
3/4 c. brown sugar	1/2 c. chopped nuts
1/4 c. corn syrup	

Roll the dough into a 9x15 rectangle. Spread the following ingredients on the dough:

1/4 c. soft butter	3/4 c. brown sugar
1 tbsp. cinnamon	1 c. washed raisins

Roll up like a jelly roll and cut into one-inch slices. Let rise until buns fill the pan. Bake at 375° for about 40 minutes. Cool for 3 minutes. Then remove from pan, upside down.

JOHNNY CAKE (CORN BREAD)

1 c. corn meal	4 tsp. baking powder
1 c. flour	1 egg
1/4 c. sugar	1 c. milk
1/2 tsp. salt	1/4 c. soft shortening

Preheat oven to 375°. Stir together and bake for 25-30 minutes at 375°.

Lydia Troyer

OVERNIGHT ROLLS

2-1/2 c. warm water
2 pkg. dry yeast
1/3 c. shortening
1/2 c. sugar

2 eggs, beaten
1 tbsp. salt
7-1/2 to 8 c. flour

Mix yeast and warm water. Beat together eggs, sugar, salt and shortening. Add to yeast mixture. Add 4 cups flour and beat; then stir in rest of flour. Dough will be soft. Do not knead. Place in a bowl and cover tightly. Store in a cold place overnight. The dough will keep for a week in the refrigerator. If you want rolls for dinner, form them in the morning and put in a warm place to rise. Bake at 350° until golden brown.

Emma Beachey

TEA ROLLS

1/4 c. warm water
3/4 c. scalded milk
1/4 c. Crisco
1 egg

1-1/2 pkg. dry yeast
1/4 c. sugar
1 tsp. salt
3-1/2 c. flour

Mix yeast and warm water and let stand. Mix sugar, Crisco, salt and egg. Pour hot milk over mixture and let cool. Add yeast, water and flour. Roll out on floured board and spread with the following:

2 tbsp. butter
2 tsp. cinnamon

1/2 c. brown sugar or
white sugar

Preheat oven to 350°. Roll up and form one ring. Make cuts about 1-1/2 in. wide all around with scissors. Bake at 350° about 30 minutes.

Mrs. John E. Miller

EARLY BIRD COFFEE CAKE

2 1/2 c. all purpose flour
2 tsp. baking powder
1/2 tsp. soda
1/2 tsp. cinnamon
1/2 tsp. nutmeg

2 c. brown sugar
2/3 c. shortening
1 c. buttermilk or sour milk
2 eggs

Preheat oven to 375°. Sift first six ingredients into mixing bowl. Cut in sugar and shortening until crumbly. Reserve one cup for topping. Stir in milk and egg just until flour is moistened. Pour batter into greased 9x9 pan. Sprinkle reserved crumb mixture over batter. Bake at 375° for 35-40 minutes.

Mrs. John C. Fisher

SUNSHINE COFFEE CAKE

Filling/Topping:
1/2 c. brown sugar
2 tsp. cinnamon
2 tbsp. flour

2 tbsp. melted butter
1/2 c. chopped nuts

Blend above ingredients together before mixing coffee cake batter.

Batter:
1-1/2 c. flour
3 tsp. baking powder
1/4 tsp. salt
3/4 c. sugar

1/4 c. shortening
1 egg
1/2 c. milk

Preheat oven to 375°. Sift dry ingredients together and cut in shortening. Beat eggs well and add milk. Combine liquid with dry ingredients. Spread half the batter in a greased flat pan 8x8 or 6x10 in. Sprinkle with half of filling. Add the other half of the batter and sprinkle with remaining filling on top. Bake at 375° for 25 minutes. Cut in squares.

Kathryn Hostetler

NOTES ON FAVORITE RECIPES

Cakes, Pies & Puddings

NOTES ON FAVORITE RECIPES

POUND CAKE

2/3 c. butter
1-1/4 c. sugar
2/3 c. milk
1 tsp. vanilla

2 c. sifted flour
1 tsp. salt
1/2 tsp. baking powder
3 eggs

Preheat oven to 300°
Cream butter and sugar. Add milk and vanilla. Blend well. Sift dry ingredients and add to creamed mixture. Beat thoroughly. Add eggs one at a time and beat well after each one. Pour into well greased loaf pan. Bake at 300° for one hour and 25 minutes. Serve with sauce or butter.

DELICATE LEMON SQUARES

1/2 c. butter
1/4 c. powdered sugar

1 c. sifted flour

Preheat oven to 325°.
Mix all ingredients. Pat into a 9" square pan. Bake at 325° for 15 minutes.

Filling;

1 c. sugar
2 tbsp. flour
1/2 tsp. baking powder

juice of 1 large lemon
2 eggs, slightly beaten

Combine all ingredients. Pour over baked layer. Bake at 325° for 25 minutes. Cool. Sprinkle with powdered sugar. Cut into squares.

CHOCOLATE SALAD DRESSING CAKE

2 c. flour

1 c. sugar

4 tbsp. cocoa

2 tsp. soda

1/2 tsp. salt

1 tsp. vanilla

1 c. salad dressing(scant)

    (like Miracle Whip)

Preheat oven to 325°.

Combine dry ingredients. Add vanilla, water and salad dressing and beat well. Bake at 325° for 35 minutes or until inserted toothpick comes out clean.

Mrs. John R. Schmucker

FRENCH SILK CHOCOLATE PIE

1/2 c. butter

3/4 c. sugar

1 sq. chocolate,

   melted and cooled

1 tsp. vanilla

2 eggs

1 pie shell, baked

Cream butter and sugar together. Blend in chocolate and vanilla. Add eggs one at a time, beating well after each addition. Pour into pie shell. Chill. Top with whipped cream and/or nuts.

Mrs. John R. Schmucker

WALNUT WONDER CAKE

2 c. flour
1 tsp. baking powder
1/2 tsp. soda
1/8 tsp. salt

1/2 c. margarine
1 c. milk
1 c. sugar

Preheat oven to 350°.
Cream sugar and margarine. Sift dry ingredients together and then add alternately to the creamed mixture with the milk. Beat well after each addition. Pour half of batter into greased 9x13 pan. Sprinkle half of topping across the batter and then add the rest of the batter. Finish by sprinkling the remainder of the topping over the top.

Topping:
1/2 c. brown sugar
1/4 c. white sugar

2 tsp. cinnamon
1/2 c. nuts

Mix together well.

Bake at 350° for 30-35 minutes.

Mrs. Mervin Detweiler

APPLE DUMPLINGS

Dough:
2 c. flour
2-1/2 tsp. baking powder
1/2 tsp. salt

2/3 c. shortening
1/2 c. milk
6 apples

Mix flour, baking powder and salt. Cut in shortening until the size of peas. Add milk and work to make a pastry. Roll and cut into 6-7 inch squares. Place apple on each square and bring corners up to make dumpling.
(continued)

Sauce:

2 c. brown sugar   1/4 c. butter
2 c. water   1/2 tsp. cinnamon

Heat sauce on top of stove. Place sauce in rectangular baking pan. Place apple dumplings in sauce and bake at 425° for 40 minutes. Keep spooning sauce over apples until brown and tender.

Mrs. Rebecca Miller

BLACK MAGIC CAKE

1-3/4 c. flour   1/2 c. vegetable oil
2 c. sugar   2 eggs
3/4 c. cocoa   1 c. strong coffee
2 tsp. baking soda   1 tsp. vanilla
1 tsp. baking powder   1 c. buttermilk
1 tsp. salt

Preheat oven to 350°.
Combine flour, sugar, cocoa, soda, baking powder and salt in large bowl. Add eggs, coffee, buttermilk and vanilla. Beat at medium speed for 2 minutes. Batter will be thin. Pour batter into a greased and floured 13x9x2 inch pan or two 9 inch cake pans. Bake at 350° for 35 to 40 minutes for oblong pan or 30 to 35 minutes for layer pans.

Mrs. Susan Weaver

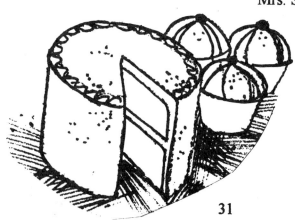

QUICK CREAM CHEESE PIE

1 8 oz. pkg. cream cheese   1 c. whipped cream
1 c. sugar

Beat sugar into cream cheese. add 1 c. whipped cream. Pour into baked pie shell. Cover with cherries or your favorite berries. Chill before serving.

Mrs. Elmer E. Yoder

RHUBARB CAKE

1/2 c. sugar   1 tsp. cinnamon
2 c. finely cut rhubarb   1 tsp. baking soda
1/2 c. butter   1/2 tsp. salt
1-1/2 c. sugar   1 c. buttermilk
1 egg   1/2 c. each coconut,
2 c. plus 2 tbsp. flour   nuts and raisins

Preheat oven to 350°.
Mix 1/2 c. sugar with rhubarb. Set aside. Blend butter, 1-1/2 c. sugar, egg and vanilla together. Mix together flour, cinnamon, soda and salt. Add alternately to butter mixture with buttermilk. Add rhubarb mixture, nuts, coconut and raisins and blend together. Pour into a greased 7x12 inch pan. Bake at 350° for 45 minutes.

Mrs. Ervin E. Miller

FAVORITE CHOCOLATE CAKE

2 c. sugar
2 c. flour
1/2 c. cocoa
2 tsp. baking soda
1 tsp. baking powder
1 tsp. salt

1 tsp. vanilla
1/2 c. vegetable oil
2 eggs
1 c. milk
1 c. hot water

Preheat oven to 350°. Mix dry ingredients. Add remaining ingredients in order given. Pour in greased 14x9 pan. Bake at 350° until a toothpick comes out clean.

FRUIT CAKE

1 pound dates
1 pound shelled mixed nuts
1 pound walnuts
1/2 pound dry cherries
1-1/2 c. flour

1 tsp. baking powder
1 c. brown sugar
4 large eggs
1 tsp. vanilla
1/2 tsp. salt

Preheat oven to 375°. Mix fruit and nuts in bowl. Sprinkle flour, sugar, salt and baking powder over fruit and nuts. Mix well. Add beaten eggs and mix. Bake at 375° for 1 hour.

Mrs. Ervin Miller

PINEAPPLE CAKE

1/2 c. Crisco oil
2-1/2 c. flour
1-1/2 c. sugar
1 tsp. vanilla

2 eggs
1-1/2 tsp. soda
1 no. 2 can crushed
    pineapple

Preheat oven to 350°. Put all ingredients together in a sauce pan and beat well. Pour into a 9x13 inch pan well greased and floured. Bake at 350° for 40 minutes. Cool and serve with Cool Whip or Dream Whip.

LOVE LIGHT MAPLE NUT CAKE

2 eggs (separated)
1/2 c. sugar
2-1/2 c. cake flour
3 tsp. baking powder
1 tsp. salt

1 c. brown sugar (packed)
1/3 c. Wesson oil
1 c. milk
1 tsp. maple flavoring
1/2 c. chopped nuts

Preheat oven to 350°. Beat egg whites until fluffy. Gradually beat in white sugar. Continue beating untill very stiff and glossy. Sift flour, baking powder and salt in another bowl. Add brown sugar, oil and half of milk. Beat 1 minute or 150 vigorous strokes by hand. Scrape sides of bowl often. Add remaining milk, egg yolks and flavoring. Beat 1 more minute. Fold in meringue and bake 30 to 35 minutes at 350°.

Laura Miller

NEVER FAIL CHOCOLATE CAKE

1-1/2 c. flour
1 c. sugar
1/2 tsp. salt
1 tsp. soda
1/2 c. cocoa

1 egg
1/2 c. shortening
1/2 c. sour milk
1/2 c. hot water
1 tbsp. vanilla

Preheat oven to 350°. Mix all ingredients together in a bowl. Add hot water last and beat for 2 minutes. Bake at 350° for 30 to 35 minutes.

Mrs. Allen Mullet

EASY MIX COCOA CAKE

3 c. flour
2 c. sugar
2/3 c. cocoa
1-1/2 tsp. salt
2 tsp. soda dissolved in
   1 c. boiling water.

1 c. sour milk
1 c. salad oil
2 eggs
2 tsp. vanilla

Preheat oven to 350°. Sift dry ingredients together. Add other ingredients as listed and mix well. Pour into two greased, floured 9 inch layer pans and bake at 350° for 30-35 minutes or until done. Do not overbake for moist cake.

Barbara Weaver

CHOCOLATE FUDGE CAKE

1/2 c. butter
1/2 c. shortening
2 c. sugar
2 eggs
1 tsp. vanilla

1/2 c. Hershey's cocoa
2-1/4 c. flour
1-1/4 tsp. baking soda
1/2 tsp. salt
1-1/3 c. water

Preheat oven to 350°. Cream butter, shortening and sugar in large mixer bowl. Add eggs and vanilla and blend well. Combine dry ingredients and add alternately with water to creamed mixture. Pour into two greased and floured 9 in. round layer pans or two 8 inch square pans. Bake at 350° until cake tester comes out clean.

Laura Miller

CHOCOLATE FUDGE FROSTING

1/3 c. butter   1/3 c. milk
1/3 c. Hershey's cocoa   1 tsp. vanilla
2-2/3 c. confectioners sugar

Melt butter in saucepan over medium heat. Add cocoa and heat just until mixture begins to boil, stirring constantly until smooth. Pour into small mixer bowl and cool completely. Add confectioners sugar alternately with milk, beating to spreading consistency. Blend in vanilla.

COCONUT PECAN FROSTING

1 c. Pet milk   1 tsp. vanilla
1 c. sugar   1-1/3 c. coconut
3 egg yolks   1 c. chopped pecans
1/4 lb. butter

Mix milk, eggs, butter and vanilla together. Cook and stir over medium heat until thickened, about 12 minutes. Add coconut and pecans. Beat until thick enough to spread.

Mrs. William W. Hochstetler

FRUIT COBBLER

1/2 c. butter   1 c. milk
1 c. sugar   1 qt. drained berries
2 c. flour   3/4 c. sugar
4 tsp. baking powder   2 c. fruit juice
1/2 tsp. salt   whipped cream

Preheat oven to 400°. Cream butter and 1 c. sugar until light and fluffy. Sift together flour, baking powder and salt. Stir dry
(continued next page)

ingredients into butter mixture alternately with milk. Pour into greased 9x13x2 loaf pan. Spoon drained berries (strawberries, blueberries, raspberries or peaches) over the top. Sprinkle with 3/4 c. sugar. Pour 2 cups fruit juice over top. Bake for 45 to 50 minutes at 400°. Serve warm with whipped cream. (Note: canned fruits are best.)

Mrs. Melvin C. Miller

QUICK CARAMEL FROSTING

1/2 c. butter, melted	1/4 c. milk
1 c. brown sugar, packed	2 c. powdered sugar

Melt butter in saucepan. Add brown sugar. Cook for 2 minutes, stirring constantly. Add milk and bring to a boil. Remove from heat and cool. Add powdered sugar. Beat well.

Esther Schmucker

MAHOGANY CHIFFON CAKE

3/4 c. boiling water	1/2 c. vegetable oil
1/2 c. cocoa	7 unbeaten egg yolks
1-3/4 c. softasilk flour	(medium)
1-3/4 c. sugar	2 tsp. vanilla
1-1/2 tsp. soda	1 c. egg whites (7 or 8)
1 tsp. salt	1/2 tsp. cream of tartar

Heat oven to 325°. Combine boiling water and cocoa and let cool. Blend sugar, flour, soda and salt in bowl. Make a well and add oil, egg yolks, vanilla and cocoa mixture. Beat until smooth. Measure egg whites and cream of tartar into large mixing bowl and beat until very stiff. Pour egg yolk mixture in thin stream over entire surface of egg whites, gently cutting and folding in with rubber spatula until blended. Bake 55 minutes at 325°, then 10 to 15 minutes at 350°. Invert to cool.

Ella M. Byler

MILE-A-MINUTE CUPCAKES

1/2 c. shortening	1/2 tsp. soda
1 c. sugar	1/2 c. cocoa
2 eggs	1 c. milk
2 c. flour	1 tsp. vanilla
1/4 tsp. salt	1/2 c. hot coffee
1 tsp. baking powder	

Preheat oven to 375°. Cream shortening, sugar, eggs. Add flour, salt, baking powder, soda, cocoa mixed in milk, vanilla and coffee. Mix well. Bake at 375° for 20 minutes. Makes 2 dozen.

Mrs. Ervin E. C. Miller

JELLY ROLL

4 egg yolks	1 c. flour
2 tbsp. water	1 tsp. baking powder
1 c. sugar	2/3 c. jam or jelly
1 tsp. vanilla	powdered sugar
pinch of salt	

Heat oven to 375°. Line jelly roll pan 15-1/2x10-1/2x1 inch with aluminum foil or waxed paper. Grease generously. Beat eggs and water together until smooth. Add sugar, vanilla and salt and beat well. Add flour and baking powder and beat until batter is smooth. Beat egg whites until fluffy and fold into batter. Bake about 12 to 15 minutes. Loosen cake from edges of pan and invert on towel sprinkled generously with powdered sugar. Carefully remove waxed paper or foil. While hot, carefully roll cake and towel from narrow end. Cool on wire rack at least 30 minutes. Unroll cake and remove towel. Beat jelly to make it smooth and spread over cake. Roll up and sprinkle with powdered sugar. Makes 10 servings.

Mrs. W. J. S. Miller

MAPLE NUT CHIFFON CAKE

2-1/4 c. flour
3/4 c. granulated sugar
3 tsp. baking powder
1/2 tsp. salt
3/4 c. brown sugar
1/2 c. salad oil

5 egg yolks
3/4 c. cold water
2 tsp. maple flavoring
5 egg whites
1/2 tsp. cream of tartar
1 c. nuts

Preheat oven to 325°. Sift flour, sugar, baking powder and salt into mixing bowl. Stir in brown sugar and make a well in dry ingredients. In this order add salad oil, egg yolks, water and flavoring. Beat until satin smooth. Combine egg whites and cream of tartar in large mixing bowl. Beat until stiff (stiffer than angel food). Pour egg yolk batter in thin stream over entire surface of egg whites, gently cutting and folding down across bottom, up the side, and over just until blended. Fold in nuts. Bake in ungreased tube pan at 325° for 55 minutes. Increase heat to 350° and bake 15 minutes longer. Cool. Frost with maple flavored frosting.

Kathryn Hostetler

CHOCOLATE SHEET CAKE

2 c. flour
2 c. sugar
1/2 c. oil
1 stick butter or margarine
1 c. water

4 tbsp. cocoa
1/2 c. buttermilk
2 eggs
1 tsp. soda
1 tsp. vanilla

Preheat oven to 400°. Sift flour and sugar together. Bring to boil; oil, butter, water and cocoa. Mix these with flour and sugar. Add buttermilk, eggs, soda and vanilla. Bake at 400° for 15 to 18 minutes. Cook icing while cake is baking and ice cake while still hot:

(continued on next page)

Icing:

1/2 c. butter	1 box confectioners sugar
4 tbsp. cocoa	4 tbsp. buttermilk
1 tsp. vanilla	2 c. walnuts

Bring butter, cocoa and vanilla to boil. Mix with sugar, buttermilk and walnuts.

Esther Schmucker

SHORTCAKE FOR STRAWBERRIES

2-1/4 c. cake flour	1/3 c. shortening
4 tsp. baking powder	1 egg
2 tbsp. sugar	2/3 c. milk
1/2 tsp. salt	

Preheat oven to 425°. Sift flour, baking powder, salt and sugar together. Add shortening, cutting in with a pastry blender until crumbly. Stir in egg and milk. Spread in greased, 8 in. round cake pan. Bake at 425° for 15 minutes.

Edna D. Yoder

TAWNY GOLD FROSTING

2 egg whites - unbeaten	3 tbsp. dark or light Karo
1 c. sugar	1/4 tsp. cream of tartar
1/2 c. brown sugar	pinch of salt
2 tbsp. water	1 tsp. vanilla

Cook in double boiler until sugars dissolve; then beat with rotary beater until thick and spread able.

Mrs. Urie M. Byler

SEVEN-MINUTE FROSTING

2 egg whites - unbeaten   1 tsp. corn syrup or
1-1/2 c. granulated sugar   1/4 tsp. cream of tartar
5 tbsp. cold water   1 tsp. vanilla

Combine egg whites, sugar, water and corn syrup in the top of
double boiler. Mix thoroughly. Place over rapidly boiling water
and beat constantly with rotary beater until mixture will hold a
peak. This requires approximately 7 minutes. Remove from
heat. Add vanilla and beat until thick enough to spread.

Kathryn Hostetler

PINEAPPLE SHEET CAKE

Filling:
1 can (no. 2-1/2) crushed   2/3 c. sugar
   pineapple   2 tbsp. corn starch

Dough:
2/3 c. warm milk   3 beaten egg yolks
4 tsp. sugar   3 c. flour
1 cake yeast   1/2 lb. margarine

Preheat oven to 350°. Combine crushed pineapple, sugar and
cornstarch in pan. Cook until thick. Cool. Cut margarine into
flour as for pie dough; crumble yeast into milk and add sugar.
Let stand until mixture bubbles; add to flour mixture. Mix
beaten egg yolks. Knead dough lightly and divide into two
parts. Roll out one half of dough on floured board to fit pan
9x13 in. Spread pineapple mixture on top. Roll out second
piece of dough and place on top of filling. Let stand for 1 hour
in warm place. Bake in 350° oven for 30 minutes. At once put
on thin confectioners sugar frosting. Other fillings such as
blueberry and raspberry may be used instead of pineapple.

Mrs. Harvey W. Byler

CREAM SAUCE FOR ANGEL FOOD CAKE

1/4 c. butter	1 egg
1-1/2 c. sugar	1 tsp. vanilla
1/2 c. milk	

Put all ingredients in saucepan and boil for 3 minutes. Spoon over Angel Food cake slices when cool.

SALAD DRESSING CAKE

1 c. sugar	1/8 tsp. salt
1 c. salad dressing	4 tsp. cocoa
2 c. flour	1 c. water
2 tsp. soda-scant	1 tsp. vanilla

Preheat oven to 375°. Mix all ingredients together. Pour into a greased 9x13 in. pan or two 8 in. layer pans. Bake at 375° for 30-40 minutes.

Mrs. Rebecca Miller

RECIPE FOR LIFE

1 cup good thoughts
1 cup kind words
1 cup consideration for others
2 cups well beaten faults
3 cups forgiveness
Mix thoroughly with tears of joy,
sorrow and sympathy for others.
Fold in 4 cups of prayer and faith,
to lighten the other ingredients and
let rise, to great heights of Christian living.
After pouring all of this into your family life
bake well with the warmth of human kindness.
Serve with a smile.

SHEET CAKE

Put in saucepan:

1 stick butter	4 tbsp. cocoa
1/2 c. vegetable oil	1 c. hot water

Preheat oven to 400°.

Meanwhile, sift into mixing bowl and have ready:

2 c. flour	1 tsp. baking soda
2 c. sugar	1 tsp. salt

Add boiled cocoa mixture, beat well. Add:

2 beaten eggs	1 tsp. vanilla
1/2 c. sour milk	

Mix well. Bake in 17x11 in. pan or large cookie sheet at 400° for 15 to 20 minutes.

Icing:

Cook while cake bakes and ice immediately.

Bring to boil:

1 stick butter	1 tsp. vanilla
4 tbsp. milk or cream	

Mix with:

4 tbsp. cocoa	1/2 c. nuts (optional)
1 box powdered sugar	

Lydia Troyer

COCONUT PIE

1-1/2 c. sugar
2 eggs
1/2 tsp. salt
1-1/2 c. coconut

1/2 c. butter
1/4 c. flour
3/4 c. milk
un- baked pie shell

Preheat oven to 350°. Beat eggs, sugar and salt until lemon-colored. Add butter and flour. Blend well and add milk. Fold in 1 c. coconut. Pour in unbaked pie shell. Put remaining coconut on top. Bake one hour at 350°

Mrs. Freeman J. Miller

WACKY CAKE

Sift together:

Add:

3 c. flour
2 c. sugar
3 tbsp. cocoa
2 tsp. soda
1/2 tsp. salt

3/4 c. cooking oil
2 tbsp. vinegar
1 tbsp. vanilla
2 c. cold water

Preheat oven to 350°. Mix all ingredients together well. Pour batter into 2 greased and floured 8 in. layer pans or. a 9x13 in. pan. Bake at 350° for 45 minutes.

Mrs. Dan T. Yoder

APPLE CAKE

6 tbsp. butter
2 c. white sugar
2 eggs
2 c. flour
1 tsp. nutmeg
(continued next page)

2 tsp. soda
2 tsp. vanilla
1 tsp. salt
1 c. nuts
6 c. chopped apples

Preheat oven to 350°. Cream butter and sugar together and beat in eggs one at a time. Add dry ingredients and mix well. Add apples and nuts and mix thoroughly. Bake in a greased 13x9 in. pan for 1 hour at 350°.

Anna Marie Weaver

YELLOW PUDDING CAKE

1 yellow cake mix
1/4 c. cooking oil
1 pkg. instant pineapple
   cream pudding
2 c. milk

1 8 oz. pkg. cream cheese
1 can crushed pineapple
1 pkg. Dream Whip, whipped
chopped nuts

Preheat oven to 350°. Mix cake mix according to instructions on back of box. Add 1/4 c. cooking oil. Pour into greased pizza pan 16x11 in. and bake in 350° oven until cake is done. Cool. Mix instant pineapple cream pudding with 2 cups of milk and 1 package softened cream cheese. Drain one can crushed pineapple. Put pudding mixture on top of cake. Put crushed pineapple on top of pudding. Whip Dream Whip and put on top. Cover with chopped nuts. Chill before serving.

Ada J. Shrock

SPICE CAKE

2 c. brown sugar
1/2 c. butter
1 c. buttermilk
2 eggs
2 c. flour

1 tsp. vanilla
1 tsp. cinnamon
1 tsp. cloves
1 tsp. all spice
1 tsp. soda

Preheat oven to 350°. Cream together sugar and butter. Add buttermilk and eggs and vanilla. Stir well. Add flour and spices. Beat well. Bake in a greased loaf pan at 350° until done.

45

OATMEAL CAKE

1 c. oatmeal
1-1/4 c. boiling water
1 c. brown sugar
2 eggs, beaten
1 c. white sugar
1 stick margarine

1-1/3 c. flour
1/2 tsp. salt
1 tsp. soda
1 tsp. cinnamon
1 tsp. vanilla

Mix oatmeal with boiling water. Let stand 15 minutes. Cream shortening and sugars. Add beaten eggs and mix well. Add oatmeal to creamed mixture. Mix in dry ingredients and beat well. Pour into greased 9x13 in. rectangular pan. Bake at 350° for 25 to 30 minutes.

Topping:
1 c. brown sugar
4 tbsp. butter
1/2 c. evaporated milk

1/2 c. chopped nuts
1 c. coconut

Combine all ingredients together in a saucepan and bring to a boil. Spread on top of warm cake and put in 350° oven for 2 to 3 minutes and brown.

Mrs. Jonas Stutzman

46

AMISH CAKE

1/2 c. butter
2 c. brown sugar (packed)
2 c. buttermilk or sour milk

2 tsp. soda
3 c. flour
1 tsp. vanilla

Preheat oven to 375°. Cream butter and brown sugar. Add buttermilk, soda, flour and vanilla. Bake at 375° for about 30 minutes.

Topping:
6 tbsp. soft butter
4 tbsp. milk

1 c. brown sugar
1/2 c. nuts

Mix above ingredients and spread over cake. Return cake to oven and bake until topping is bubbly.

Edna Mullet

SOFT GINGERBREAD

1/2 c. butter
1/4 c. sugar
1 c. molasses
1 tbsp. cinnamon
1 tsp. ginger

2-1/2 c. flour
2 tsp. soda
1 c. boiling water
2 eggs, beaten

Preheat oven to 350°. Cream butter, sugar, molasses, cinnamon and ginger together. Beat well and add flour and soda dissolved in water. Mix well. Add beaten eggs. Pour into greased 9x9 in square cake pan and bake at 350° for 40 to 45 minutes.

Sovilla Miller

SPONGE SHORTCAKE

3 eggs
1 c. sugar
6 tbsp. cold water
pinch of salt

1 tsp. vanilla
1 c. flour
1-1/2 tsp. baking powder

Preheat oven to 350°. Beat eggs and water until thick and lemon colored. Add sugar. Add dry ingredients. Mix and bake at 350° in a 9x9 square cake pan for 30-35 minutes. Serve with fresh strawberries, topped with whipped cream.

Mrs. Eli Wengerd

CHOCOLATE MAYONNAISE CAKE

2 c. flour
1 c. sugar
1/2 c. cocoa
2 tsp. soda

1 c. boiling water
1 tsp. vanilla
1 c. mayonnaise

Sift together flour, sugar, cocoa and soda. Mix all together with other ingredients. Pour batter into a greased and floured 9x13 in. pan or two 8 in. layer pans. Bake in 325-350° oven for 45 minutes.

Mrs. Owen Schmucker

PRINCE OF WALES CAKE

1 egg, beaten
1/2 c. Crisco
1 c. sugar
1 c. sour milk or buttermilk
2 tbsp. molasses

1 tsp. baking soda
1 tsp. cinnamon
1/2 tsp. cloves
2 c. flour
1/2 tsp. salt

Preheat oven to 350°. Cream Crisco, add sugar and beaten egg. Combine dry ingredients. Dissolve baking soda in sour milk. Alternately add dry ingredients and sour milk to creamed Crisco mixture. Beat well. Pour into greased loaf pan and bake at 350° until it springs back when touched with finger.

Mrs. W. J. Hochstetler

YARD LOAF CAKE

12 tbsp. shortening
3 c. brown sugar
2 tsp. cinnamon
1 tsp. cloves
1 tsp. allspice

2 tsp. soda
3 c. flour
1 c. raisins
2 c. sour milk

Preheat oven to 375°. Cream shortening and sugar. Sift dry ingredients together. Add dry ingredients alternately with sour milk to creamed mixture. Mix well. Pour into greased 9x13 in. pan and bake at 375° for 35 to 40 minutes.

Mrs. Elmer Dan Yoder

ANGEL FOOD CAKE

1-1/2 c. egg whites (11-12)   1 c. cake flour
1-1/2 c. white sugar   1/2 tsp. salt
1-1/2 tsp. cream of tartar   1 tsp. almond flavor

Preheat oven to 375°. Sift together 3/4 c. of sugar and the 1 c. of flour three times. Set aside. Beat egg whites until frothy, then add salt and cream of tartar. Beat until it stands in peaks. Add rest of sugar about 3 tbsp. at a time, beating well with a beater after each addition. Lightly fold in sugar and flour mixture, adding about 1/2 c. at a time. Add almond flavoring. Bake at 375° about 35-40 minutes in a tube pan.

Katherine M. Byler

BIG WALNUT CAKE

1-1/4 c. walnuts, chopped   1 c. shortening
3-1/2 c. cake flour   1 tsp. almond extract
5 tsp. baking powder   1 tsp. vanilla
1 tsp. salt   1-1/2 c. sugar
1-1/2 c. milk   4 egg yolks, beaten
4 egg whites   1/4 c. sugar

Preheat oven to 350°. Sift together cake flour, baking powder and salt. Set aside. Cream shortening, almond extract, vanilla, 1-1/2 c. sugar and egg yolks. Add dry ingredients alternately to creamed mixture with milk. Beat until smooth, after each addition, ending with flour. Beat egg whites until fluffy and add 1/4 c. sugar. Fold the egg whites slowly into the cake batter. Add nuts and pour into greased, floured pans. Make 3 layers. Bake at 350° for 30-35 minutes.

Mrs. Joseph J. Weaver

BOILED FRUIT CAKE

1 c. sugar	1 tsp. cinnamon
1 c. raisins	1/4 tsp. nutmeg
1 c. boiling water	1/2 tsp. salt
1/2 c. shortening	1 tsp. soda
1/2 tsp. cloves	2 c. flour

Mix all ingredients together, except for soda and flour. Boil for 5 minutes. Let cool. When cold, add soda and flour. Pour into greased bread pan and bake at 350° (moderate oven) until a toothpick comes out clean.

Emma Beachey

LAZY WIFE CAKE

1-1/2 c. pastry flour	3 tbsp. cocoa
1/4 tsp. salt	1 c. white sugar
2 tsp. soda	1 tbsp. cooking oil
1 tsp. vanilla	(plus a bit)
1 c. water	1 tbsp. vinegar

Preheat oven to 350°. Sift all dry ingredients into a 9x9 in. ungreased cake pan. Mix with a fork. Make three holes in the dry ingredients. Into one hole put the vanilla, next the oil, third the vinegar. Pour water in pan over other ingredients. Mix with a fork. Do not beat. Bake at 350° for 25 minutes.

Edna Mullet

CRAZY CHOCOLATE CAKE

3 c. flour
2 c. sugar
1/2 c. cocoa
2 tsp. baking powder
2 tsp. baking soda

1 tsp. salt
2 eggs
2/3 c. shortening
1 c. sour milk
1-1/4 c. boiling water

Preheat oven to 350°. Combine dry ingredients and sift into large mixing bowl. Add eggs, shortening, sour milk and boiling water. Stir until moistened. Beat until smooth. Pour into greased 9x13 in. pan. Bake in 350° for 30-35 minutes. Cool and frost.

Barbara Miller

BLACK MAGIC CAKE

2 c. sugar
2 c. flour
1/2 c. cocoa
2 tsp. soda
1/2 tsp. salt

1/2 c. vegetable oil
2 eggs
1/2 c. milk
1 tsp. vanilla
1 c. hot water

Preheat oven to 350°. Mix sugar, flour, cocoa, soda and salt. Add shortening, eggs, milk and vanilla. Mix well. Add hot water and mix again. Pour into greased pans and bake at 350°.

Mrs. Freeman J. Miller

FRENCH CREAM CAKE

1 c. sugar	2 tsp. baking powder
3 eggs	1/2 tsp. salt
1-1/2 c. flour	3 tbsp. water

Preheat oven to 350°. Beat eggs and sugar until light and fluffy. Slowly add dry ingredients. Add water last. Beat well. Bake in greased layer pans at 350° for 30-35 minutes. Cool.

Filling:

2 c. milk	2 eggs, beaten
2 tbsp. cornstarch	1 c. sugar

Mix cornstarch with small amount of cold milk, beaten eggs and sugar. Cook until thick. Cool. Slice layers sideways and spread filling between layers, but not on top. Dust top with confectioner's sugar.

Mrs. William J. Hochstetler

THE FARMER'S LOVE LETTER

My sweet potato, do you carrot all for me?
You are the apple of my eye.
With your radish hair and turnip nose,
my heart beets for you.

My love for you is as strong as onions.
If we cantaloupe, lettuce marry,
and we'll be a happy pear.

Mrs. Robert Gingerich

STEAMED APPLE PUDDING

1-1/2 c. sifted all-purpose flour
1 tsp. baking soda
1/2 tsp. salt
1/2 tsp. cinnamon
1/2 tsp. nutmeg
1/4 tsp. cloves
light cream

1/4 c. soft butter or margarine
1 c. sugar
2 eggs, well beaten
4 pared medium apples, shredded (2-1/2 c.)
1/2 c. dark raisins

Grease well a 1-1/2 qt. heat proof bowl. Into small bowl, sift flour with baking soda, salt and spices and set aside. In large bowl with wooden spoon beat butter, sugar and eggs until mixture is smooth and light. Stir in apples and raisins. Stir flour mixture into the fruit mixture, mixing well and turn into greased bowl. Cover surface of pudding with double thickness of waxed paper. Cover top of bowl completely with foil and tie edge securely with twine. Place bowl on trivet in large kettle. Pour boiling water around bowl to come halfway up side. Cover kettle and bring to boiling. Reduce heat and boil gently for two hours.

Mrs. Eileen Miller

APPLE GOODIE

Base:

1-1/2 c. sugar

2 tbsp. flour

pinch of salt

1 tsp. cinnamon

1-1/2 qt. sliced apples

Mix sugar, flour, salt and cinnamon. Add to apples and mix. Put in bottom of greased cake pan.

Topping:

1 c. oatmeal

1 c. brown sugar

1 c. flour

1/4 tsp. soda

1/3 tsp. baking powder

2/3 c. butter

Mix together until crumbly and place evenly on top of apples and pat firmly. Bake at 375° until brown and crust is formed. Serve with milk or cream.

Mrs. Ervin E. Miller

EXTRA MOIST CHOCOLATE CAKE

2-1/2 c. all purpose flour

2 c. sugar

1 tsp. baking powder

4 tbsp. cocoa

1/4 tsp. salt

2 eggs

1 c. salad oil

1 c. buttermilk or sour milk

1 tsp. vanilla

1 tsp. soda

1 c. hot water

Preheat oven to 350°. Sift dry ingredients in mixing bowl. Add eggs, salad oil, buttermilk and vanilla and beat well. Dissolve 2 tsp. soda in 1 c. hot water and add. Beat again. Batter will be thin. Bake at 350° for 35 to 45 minutes.

Mrs. Emma Yoder

APPLE CAKE

2 c. apples, sliced	1 c. sugar
1/4 c. cooking oil	1 egg
1 c. flour	1 tsp. soda
1 tsp. flour	1/4 tsp. salt
1 tsp. cinnamon	1 tsp. vanilla

Preheat oven to 350°. Mix apples and sugar in bowl and let stand 10 minutes. Add oil and egg and mix well. Add dry ingredients and stir in vanilla. Bake in 8" or 9" cake pan. Bake at 350° for 45 to 50 minutes. About halfway through baking time cake may be sprinkled with mixture of:

2 tbsp. sugar	1 tsp. cinnamon

May be served with or without Cool Whip, as desired.

Mrs. Rebecca Miller

FRUIT COCKTAIL TORTE

1 egg	1 tsp. soda
1 1 lb. can fruit cocktail	1/2 tsp. salt
1 c. flour	1 c. brown sugar
1 c. sugar	1 c. nuts

Beat egg and add fruit with juice. Add dry ingredients and mix well. Pour into greased 9x9 in pan. Sprinkle with brown sugar and nuts. Bake at 350° for 40 minutes. Serve with whipped cream.

Barbara Miller

HOT FUDGE PUDDING

1 c. flour
2 tsp. baking powder
1/4 tsp. salt
3/4 c. sugar
2 tbsp. cocoa
1-3/4 c. hot water

1/2 c. milk
2 tbsp. vegetable oil
1 c. chopped nuts
1 c. brown sugar
1/4 c. cocoa

Preheat oven to 350°. Sift together in a bowl: flour, baking powder, salt, sugar and 2 tbsp. cocoa. Stir in milk, vegetable oil and nuts. Pour into 9 in. square pan. Sprinkle with brown sugar and 1/4 c. cocoa. Pour hot water over entire mixture. Bake in 350° oven for 45 minutes. Cake mixture will rise to top. Serve with or without whipped cream.

Esther Schmucker

CHOCOLATE ICEBOX PUDDING

1/2 lb. sweet baking
   chocolate
2 tbsp. hot water
3 tbsp. sugar

1 tsp. vanilla
1/2 c. whipped cream
1 pkg. vanilla wafers
4 eggs separated

Melt chocolate with hot water in a double boiler. Add sugar and egg yolks. Cool at once. Add nuts and vanilla. Fold in egg whites and whipping cream. Line bottom of dish with wafers and then chocolate mixture. Top with whipped cream and nuts.

Edna Mullet

EAGLE BRAND MILK PUDDING

1 can Eagle Brand milk   whipped cream
1 can pineapple slices   maraschino cherries

Boil Eagle Brand milk for 1-1/2 hours or 2 hours in water, have the can of milk covered in water all the time you are boiling it. Cool. Open both ends and push out of can and slice onto pineapple slices. Top with a dab of whipped cream and garnish with a maraschino cherry.

Mrs. E. F. Miller

LEMON DESSERT

1 stick of soft margarine   1/2 c. finely chopped
1 c. flour   walnuts

Mix all together and put into 9x13 in. pan. Bake 15 minutes at 350°. Cool completely before adding next layer.

1 c. powdered sugar   8 oz. cream cheese
1 c. Cool Whip   (whipped)

Mix above ingredients, beat together and spread over crust. Mix:

2 small boxes lemon   3 c. milk
   instant pudding

Beat on low speed until thick. Spread on top of cream cheese mixture. Top this with Cool Whip and sprinkle with nuts. You can also use other flavors of pudding. Try fresh sliced peaches on top of cream cheese mixture. Then top with vanilla pudding, then Cool Whip. Chill.

Mrs. Susan Weaver

PISTACHIO PUDDING

1 can crushed pineapple
1 c. marshmallows,
   colored

1 c. nuts, chopped
1 small Cool Whip
1 pkg. instant Pistachio
   Pudding

Mix all together and chill before serving.

DATE PUDDING

1 c. unsifted flour
1 c. sugar
1 c. chopped dates
1 c. chopped walnuts
1/2 c. milk

2 tbsp. butter
1/2 tsp. salt
1 tsp. baking powder
1 tsp. vanilla
1 egg slightly beaten

Preheat oven to 350°. Combine above ingredients and pour into greased 13x9x2 in. pan.

Sauce:
2 c. water
2 c. light brown sugar

2 tbsp. butter

Bring water to boil and stir in firmly packed brown sugar and butter. Stir until butter melts and sugar dissolves. Pour over batter in pan. Bake at 350° for 25 to 30 minutes or until center of pudding is just set.

Mrs. Jonas Stutzman

BLUEBERRY BETTY

1 qt. fresh blueberries   1/4 tsp. salt
1 tbsp. lemon juice

Combine above in bottom of 9x13 in. baking pan.

Topping:
1 c. flour   1/2 c. butter
1 c. sugar

Spread topping over base and bake at 375° for 45 minutes.

COTTAGE PUDDING

1 c. sugar   1-2/3 c. flour
3 tbsp. butter   2-1/2 tsp. baking powder
1 egg   1 tsp. vanilla
2/3 c. milk

Preheat oven to 350°. Combine above and bake in shallow pan
at 350° for 30-35 minutes. Serve with the following hot sauce:

3/4 c. butter   1 c. sugar
4 tbsp. flour   1 tsp. vanilla

Brown butter and sugar until a rich golden brown. Add flour,
stir in enough water to make like gravy and boil. Remove from
heat, add vanilla.

Mrs. Raymond M. Miller

BANANA SPLIT DESSERT

2 c. graham cracker crumbs
1 stick margarine, melted
2 c. powdered sugar
2 sticks margarine
2 eggs
2 tsp. vanilla
7 bananas
2 cans crushed pineapple
2 pkgs. Cool Whip
Chopped nuts and cherries

Mix 1 stick of melted margarine with graham cracker crumbs and press into 9x13 in. cake pan. Beat powdered sugar and margarine together. Add eggs and vanilla and beat until light and fluffy. Spread on graham cracker crust. Spread sliced bananas and drained pineapple across top. Top with Cool Whip, nuts and cherries and refrigerate.

Mrs. Chris Troyer

ICE CREAM PUDDING

1/2 lb. Hershey candy bars
2 tbsp. hot water
3 tbsp. sugar
4 egg yolks
1/2 tsp. salt
1/2 c. nuts
1/2 tsp. vanilla
1 c. whipped cream
4 egg whites - whipped
vanilla wafers

Put candy bars and hot water in a double boiler. Melt chocolate. Add sugar, egg yolks (one at a time, mixing after each). Add salt and cool. Add nuts, vanilla, whipped cream and egg whites. Mix well and refrigerate. May be poured over layer of vanilla wafers before refrigerating.

Mrs. Sam Detweiler

PINEAPPLE DELIGHT

Bottom Part:
1 pkg. graham crackers   4 tbsp. butter, melted
   crumbled

First Layer:
2 eggs, beaten   2 c. powdered sugar
1/2 c. butter, softened

Second Layer:
1 can crushed pineapple   1/2 c. nuts
   drained
1/2 pint whipped cream,
   sweetened

Mix graham cracker crumbs with melted butter. Spread 1/2 of
the crumbs on the bottom of a round or square baking dish.
Keep rest for top. Mix eggs, butter and sugar together and
spread over crumbs in dish. Mix pineapple, whipped cream and
nuts, and spread over egg mixture. Add remaining crumbs to
top. Cool in refrigerator before serving.

Ella M. Byler

AMISH WISDOM

We pick our friends,
but do not pick them to pieces.

If everyone followed you,
completely to the letter.
Tell me, if they followed you,
Would the world be any better?

Swallow your pride occasionally.
It's non-fattening.

MISSISSIPPI MUD

1-1/2 c. brown sugar
2-1/2 c. milk
1/2 c. water
1 tsp. vanilla
3 egg whites

3 egg yolks ·
4 tbsp. flour
12 graham crackers
1 tbsp. butter

Melt butter and brown. Add sugar and water and boil until thick. Mix egg yolks, flour, and milk. Add to syrup and boil until thick. Add vanilla and put into a dish. Roll graham crackers into crumbs and spread on top. Beat egg whites until fluffy. Add enough sugar to sweeten slightly. Spread egg whites on top and sprinkle with a few crumbs. Brown lightly in a 350° oven.

Edna Mullet

LITTLE BIRD

Peck, peck, peck on my window sill.
I see a bird with a yellow bill.
He hops about and flaps his wings,
And then a merry song he sings.
To thank the bird for his merry song,
I'll scatter crumbs all winter long.

Martha Byler

PINE SCOTCH PUDDING

2 eggs
1 c. sugar
1 tsp. vanilla
1 c. crushed pineapple
   drained

3/4 c. flour
1 tsp. baking powder
1/2 tsp. salt
1 c. nuts

Preheat oven to 350°. Beat eggs until fluffy; add sugar and vanilla. Beat until thick and lemon colored. Fold in drained, crushed pineapple and nuts. Then fold in dry ingredients. Put in greased pan and bake at 350° until done.
Sauce:
1/2 c. margarine
1 tbsp. flour
1 c. brown sugar

1 egg
1/4 c. pineapple juice
1/4 c. water

Boil together 3 minutes and pour over cake before serving.

Mrs. Eli Wengerd

PARADISE PUDDING

2 tbsp. soft butter
3/4 c. powdered sugar
2 egg yolks
2/3 c. graham cracker
   crumbs

1 c. heavy cream
1 c. crushed pineapple
   drained
1/4 c. chopped nuts
2 tbsp. sugar

Cream soft butter, sugar. Add egg yolks. Spread 1/3 c. of graham cracker crumbs in a pie pan or platter. Pour egg mixture over crumbs. Cover with another 1/3 c. of crumbs.
Topping:
Whip heavy cream until stiff. Add 1 cup drained, crushed pineapple, 1/4 c. chopped nuts, 2 tbsp. sugar and vanilla to taste. Spread across top of pudding. Chill before serving.

Mrs. Elmer Dan Yoder

GRAHAM CRACKER FLUFF

1 pkg. plain gelatin	2 egg yolks
1/3 c. cold water	1 tsp. vanilla
1/2 c. sugar	2 egg whites, stiffly beaten
3/4 c. half and half	1 c. whipping cream
	whipped

Soak gelatin in 1/3 c. cold water. Mix sugar, half and half and egg yolks. Cook for 1 minute in double boiler, stirring constantly. Remove from heat, add gelatin and vanilla. Chill until mixture begins to thicken. Then add stiffly beaten egg whites and whipped cream.

Crumbs:

1-1/2 tbsp. butter	12 graham crackers,
3 tbsp. brown sugar	crushed

Melt butter and brown sugar together. Mix with crushed graham crackers. Line the bottom of a dish with 1/2 of the crumbs. Pour in pudding. Put remaining crumbs on top. Chill before serving.

Mrs. Crist Miller

TUTTI FRUITY PUDDING

1 egg	1/2 tsp. salt
1 can fruit cocktail	1 tbsp. baking powder
(#303)	1/2 c. brown sugar
1 c. flour	3/4 c. nuts, chopped
1 c. sugar	

Preheat oven to 350°. Beat eggs thoroughly. Drain fruit cocktail and save the juice. Add fruit and 1/2 c. of the juice to egg. Sift flour, sugar, salt and baking powder together. Add to egg mixture gradually. Pour into greased and floured 9x13 in. baking dish. Mix brown sugar and nuts and sprinkle over top of batter. Bake in 350° oven for 30 to 40 minutes.

Mrs. E. F. Miller

CUSTARD

5-1/2 c. warm milk   16 tbsp. sugar
8 eggs   1 tsp. salt

Preheat oven to 350°. Mix all ingredients thoroughly. Put in a large baking dish, which has been placed in a pan of water. Bake at 350° for about one hour.

Ella M. Byler

STRAWBERRY CHIFFON SQUARES

1/3 c. butter
1-1/2 c. crushed graham
    crackers
1 3 oz. pkg. strawberry
    gelatin
3/4 c. boiling water
1 14 oz. can sweetened
    condensed milk

1 10 oz. pkg. frozen
    sliced strawberries
    in syrup (thawed)
4 c. miniature marshmallows
1 c. whipping cream,
    whipped

Melt butter in pan. Stir in crumbs and mix well. Pat in baking dish 7x11 in. and chill. In a large bowl dissolve gelatin in boiling water. Add Eagle Brand milk and strawberries with juice; fold in marshmallows and whipped cream. Pour over crumbs and chill until set.

Liz Miller

BAKED CHOCOLATE FLOAT

1 c. flour	3 tbsp. cocoa
3/4 c. sugar	3 tbsp. butter
1/4 tsp. salt	1 tsp. vanilla
1 tsp. baking powder	1/2 c. nuts

Preheat oven to 350°. Sift dry ingredients together. Mix vanilla, milk, butter and nuts and add to dry ingredients. Mix well and pour into greased pan.

Sauce:

| 1/2 c. brown sugar | 3 tbsp. cocoa |
| 1/2 c. white sugar | 1 c. hot water |

Mix well and pour over batter. Bake for 40 minutes at 350°.

Lucie Byler

AMISH PUDDING

| 1 c. flour | 1 c. nuts, chopped |
| 1 stick margarine | |

Mix and spread in 9x13 in. pan (firmly). Bake at 350° for 20 minutes. When cool, add:

First Layer:

| 1 c. powdered sugar | 1 c. Cool Whip or |
| 1 8 oz. pkg. cream cheese | Dream Whip, whipped |

Spread above on pastry.

Second Layer:
1 box of chocolate instant pudding
(made according to directions on box)
Spread second layer on first layer. (Any kind of pudding can be used). Chill before serving.

Kathryn Byler

67

TROPICAL PINEAPPLE DELIGHT

1 yellow cake   4 c. milk
   (mix may be used)   1 8 oz. pkg. cream cheese
1 lg. can crushed pineapple   1 9 oz. pkg. Cool Whip
   drained   coconut for top
3 pkg. instant coconut pudding

Bake yellow cake in greased, floured 15x10 in. pan. Let cake cool. Drain pineapple and spread on top of cake. Whip together, milk, cream cheese and 3 packages instant coconut pudding. Spread this mixture over pineapple. Then spread Cool Whip over pudding mixture. Sprinkle with coconut. Chill.

Ella M. Byler

CHOCOLATE CHEESE PUDDING

1 6 oz. pkg. chocolate chips   2 eggs, separated
1 8 oz. pkg. cream cheese   1 c. heavy whipping cream
   (softened)   pinch of salt
3/4 c. sugar   1/8 tsp. vanilla

Melt chocolate over hot, not boiling water and cool for about 20 minutes. Blend cream cheese, 1/2 cup of the sugar, salt and vanilla. Beat in egg yolks one at a time. Add cooled chocolate. Blend well, beat egg whites until stiff but not dry; slowly beat in 1/4 c. sugar and beat very stiff. Fold chocolate mixture into beaten egg whites and fold in whipped cream. Line a dish with vanilla wafers and add pudding. Chill overnight. Top with chopped nuts or additional whipped cream.

Mrs. Emma Yoder

RITZ CRACKER PUDDING

20 Ritz crackers, crushed   3 egg whites
1/2 c. brown sugar   1/2 c. sugar
1/2 c. nuts   1 tsp. vanilla

Preheat oven to 350°. Beat egg whites until stiff. Add sugar and vanilla. Fold in Ritz crackers, brown sugar and nuts. Bake for about 30 minutes at 350°. Cool. Serve with whipped cream.

Mrs. Joe Weaver

CHOCOLATE ICE CREAM BARS

1/4 c. cocoa   1/4 tsp. salt
1/4 c. sugar   6 egg yolks, beaten
1-1/2 c. milk   1/3 c. sugar

Mix cocoa and sugar. Add milk. Bring to a boil. Add well beaten egg yolks to which 1/3 c. of sugar has been added. Cook until thickened.

1/2 c. margarine, melted   2 c. graham cracker
1/4 c. sugar   crumbs

Add sugar to melted margarine and add to crumbs. Press half of the crumbs in the bottom of a square or rectangular cake pan.

Topping:
2 c. whipping cream   6 egg whites, beaten
2 tsp. vanilla   1 c. sugar

Beat egg whites. Add sugar and vanilla. Whip cream. Mix whipped cream, egg whites with chocolate mixture. Pour on top of crumbs. Sprinkle remaining crumbs on top. Cover with foil and freeze overnight. Cut into bar shaped pieces to serve.

Ada J. Shrock

FRENCH CHOCOLATE PIE

1/2 c. butter
3/4 c. sugar
2 squares baking chocolate

2 eggs
2 c. Cool Whip

Cream butter and sugar. Stir in chocolate. Add eggs one at a time, beating 5 minutes after each addition. Fold in Cool Whip and pour into 9 in. baked pie shell. Chill until firm - about 2 hours.

EMMA'S PECAN PIE

1 c. white corn syrup
1/2 c. brown sugar
3 eggs - unbeaten
1 tsp. vanilla

1/4 tsp. salt
1 c. pecans
2 tbsp. melted butter

Combine everything except nuts and beat well. Add nuts. Then pour in unbaked pie crust. Bake 50 minutes in 350° oven.

Mrs. Emma Weaver

COCONUT MACAROON PIE

1-1/2 c. sugar
2 eggs
1/2 tsp. salt
1/2 c. butter

1/4 c. flour
3/4 c. milk
1-1/2 c. shredded coconut

Beat eggs, sugar, and salt until lemon-colored. Add butter and flour and blend well. Fold in 1 c. coconut and pour into unbaked pie shell. Put remaining coconut on top. Bake at 350° about 45 minutes.

Mrs. Emma Yoder

OLD-FASHIONED BUTTERSCOTCH PIE

1/2 c. butter
1 c. water
2 egg yolks

1 c. brown sugar
2-1/2 tbsp. corn starch
1-1/2 c. milk

Brown butter in pan. Then add sugar and cook together, stirring constantly until sugar is melted. Add the water, stir slowly and cook until sugar is again dissolved. Combine corn starch, egg yolks and milk and add to sugar mixture. Cook until thickened. Makes one 9 in. pie. Pour into baked pie shell and top with cream.

Mrs. Ray D. Byler

A PRAYER

God is great, God is good,
By his hand , we all are fed.
Give us Lord, our daily bread.
Amen.

Mrs. Robert Gingerich

PEANUT BUTTER PIE

2/3 c. sugar	1/3 c. creamy peanut butter
1/2 tsp. salt	3 eggs
1 c. dark corn syrup	1 c. salted peanuts

Beat sugar, salt, corn syrup, peanut butter and eggs. Stir in peanuts. Pour into unbaked pie shell. Bake in 375° oven for about 45 minutes until crust is golden brown. Cool slightly until center is firm. Chill in refrigerator and serve with whipped cream.

CREAMY PUMPKIN PIE

1 unbaked pie shell	1 tsp. cinnamon
1 16 oz. can pumpkin	1/2 tsp. salt
1 14 oz. can Eagle Brand	1/2 tsp. nutmeg
milk	1/2 tsp. ginger
2 eggs	

Combine above. Pour into unbaked pie shell. Bake 15 minutes at 425°, reduce oven to 350° and continue baking for 35 minutes. When cooled, top each slice with whipped cream.

Mary Miller

EASY BUTTER CRUNCH CRUST

1/2 c. butter	1/2 c. nuts or coconut
1/4 c. brown sugar	1 c. flour

Mix all together and spread in a shallow pan and bake at 400°. Take out and stir. Save 3/4 c. of crumbs for topping. Press rest in pie pans. Cool and fill with your favorite filling.

Mrs. John R. Schmucker

OATMEAL PIE CRUST

1 c. quick cooking oats
1/3 c. sifted flour

1/3 c. brown sugar
1/2 tsp. salt

Mix all together in bowl. Cut in 1/3 c. butter until crumbly. Press firmly on bottom and sides of 9 in. pie plate. Bake at 375° for about 15 minutes. Cool crust completely and fill with any desired cream filling.

Mrs. Ervine E. Miller

CHOCOLATE CREAM PIE

Filling:
1/2 c. cocoa
1-1/2 c. sugar
1/3 c. corn starch
1/4 tsp. salt

3 c. milk
3 tbsp. butter
1-1/2 tsp. vanilla

Cream sugar and shortening. Mix in dry ingredients. Slowly add milk. Boil until thick. Let cool.

Crust:
1 c. flour
1 stick margarine

1/2 tsp. salt
1 tsp. sugar

Mix together and press into 9 in. pie pan. Bake at 400° about 15-20 minutes. Cool and fill with chocolate cream filling. Top with whipped cream. Makes one pie. Chill before serving.

Mrs. Eli E. Wengerd

COCONUT PIE

4 eggs - beaten
1-3/4 c. sugar
1/4 c. margarine (melted)
1/2 c. self-rising flour

2 c. milk
1 tsp. vanilla
1-1/2 c. coconut

Mix all ingredients well in a bowl. Pour into well-greased pie pans. Bake 350° until golden brown. The pie forms its own crust.

Mrs. Chris Troyer

RICE KRISPY PIE

2 eggs
2/3 c. sugar
1/2 c. dark Karo
1/4 tsp. salt

1 tsp. vanilla
2 tbsp. melted butter
1 c. Rice Krispies

Beat eggs and add remaining ingredients except cereal. Fold in cereal and pour in unbaked pie shell and bake at 375° until golden brown.

Esther Schmucker

COCOA CREAM PIE

1/2 c. cocoa
1 c. sugar
1/3 c. cornstarch
1/4 tsp. salt

3 c. milk
3 tbsp. butter
1-1/2 tsp. vanilla

Combine cocoa, sugar, cornstarch and salt. Slowly add milk and cook over medium heat. Boil 1 minute and add butter and vanilla. Pour into baked pie shell and chill.

Kathryn Byler

NEVER FAIL PIE CRUST

6 c. flour   3 tsp. baking powder
2 c. shortening   1 tsp. salt
1 egg in cup, filled with water
    to 1 cup.

Mix flour, shortening, salt and baking powder until crumbly.
Add beaten egg with water. Mix (sometimes requires more
water). This dough will keep for awhile in ice box.

Kathryn Byler

SHOO FLY PIE

3/4 c. molasses   1/3 c. butter
3/4 c. cold water   1/2 tsp. nutmeg
1/2 tsp. soda   1 tsp. cinnamon
1-1/4 c. flour   1 unbaked pie shell
1/2 c. sugar

Combine molasses, water and soda and pour in pie shell.
Combine flour, sugar and spices and butter, mix together to
make a crumb consistency. Sprinkle over liquid in pie shell.
Bake 15 minutes in very hot oven at 450°. Reduce to 375° and
bake 40 minutes.

HELPFUL HINTS

*Sprinkle a little cornstarch on top of cakes to keep the frosting
from running off.*
****
*Sprinkle some powdered sugar on the cake plate to keep it from
sticking to it.*

REFRIGERATOR CHEESE CAKE

6 oz. cream cheese
1 c. white sugar
1 pkg. lemon Jell-O
1 c. boiling water
1 can Pet milk

1 tsp. vanilla
34 graham crackers,
  crushed
1/2 c. melted or soft
  butter

Mix cream cheese with sugar until fluffy. Mix lemon Jello with boiling water. Let Jello mixture cool until it begins to set and then mix with cream cheese mixture. Beat canned milk and add vanilla. Beat until fluffy and then add to other ingredients (cheese and Jello mix). Crush graham crackers and mix with melted butter. Line pan with crumbs, saving some crumbs for the top. Pour pudding in and refrigerate. Sprinkle top with crumbs.

Mrs. Jonas Stutzman

LEMON SPONGE PIE

Juice of one lemon
2/3 c. sugar
2 eggs separated

1-1/2 tbsp. flour
2/3 c. milk
2 tsp. melted ·butter

Mix sugar and flour; stir in egg yolks, milk and lemon juice. Then add egg whites stiffly beaten. Pour into unbaked pie shell and bake at 375° until done. Makes one pie.

Elizabeth Miller

RAISIN CREAM PIE

1 c. raisins	1/2 c. sugar
3/4 c. water	1 c. milk
2 tbsp. flour	2 egg yolks

Boil raisins in water until water is absorbed. Add flour, sugar and milk and let cook 5 minutes. Add well beaten egg yolks and cook until thick. Pour into baked pie shell.

Elizabeth Miller

HARVEST PIE

1/2 c. brown sugar	3/4 c. quick oats
1/2 c. white sugar	1 c. milk
1/2 c. melted butter	2 eggs, beaten
3/4 c. white corn syrup	1 c. shredded coconut

Mix together and pour into two unbaked 8 in. pie crusts. Bake at 325° to 350° for 45 minutes. Makes 2 pies.

Mrs. Emma Byler

BIG BOYS STRAWBERRY PIE

1-1/2 c. water	1 3 oz. pkg. strawberry
3/4 c. sugar	Jello
2 level tbsp. cornstarch	1 qt. strawberries

Wash and stem berries. Drain. Cook water, sugar, cornstarch until thick and clear. Add Jello and let cool 15 minutes. Lay berries in pie shell and pour glaze over top. Serve with whipped cream.

Mrs. John Miller

OPEN FACE PEACH PIE

1-1/4 c. sliced peaches,   2 round tbsp. flour
     fresh or canned   1/2 tsp. salt
1-1/4 c. sugar (half brown   1 c. whole milk
     and half white)

Place sliced peaches in unbaked crust. Mix other ingredients in order given. Pour over peaches. Bake for 10 minutes at 400° and then reduce temperate to 350° Bake until juice looks like syrup.

Fannie D. Miller

FRENCH RHUBARB PIE

1 egg   2 tbsp. flour
1 c. sugar   3/4 c. flour
1 tsp. vanilla   1/2 c. brown sugar
1 c. sliced rhubarb   1/3 c. margarine

Mix egg, sugar, vanilla, rhubarb and 2 tbsp. flour and put into a baked pie shell. Cover with mixture of 3/4 c. flour, brown sugar and margarine. Bake at 450° for 10 minutes and reduce to 350°. Continue baking at 350° for 30 minutes.

Ada J. Miller

CREAM CHEESE DESSERT

1 8 oz. pkg. cream cheese   1/2 c. sugar
1-1/2 c. crushed pineapple   1 medium sized bowl
1-1/2 c. chopped nuts   Cool Whip

Mix cream cheese and sugar until creamy. Then drain pineapple and add all the other ingredients. Chill.

Mrs. John C. Fisher

EASY PIE CRUST

1-1/2 c. all-purpose flour
2 tsp. sugar
1 tsp. salt

1/2 c. cooking oil
2 tbsp. milk

Mix ingredients and roll out or press into pans. Prick with fork and bake at 475° until lightly browned - 8 to 10 minutes. Makes one pie crust.

Mrs. John C. Fisher

DELICIOUS APPLE PIE

2 c. water
2 c. sugar (or less)
2 tbsp. butter
2 tsp. cinnamon

pinch of salt
3 heaping tbsp. clear gel
(thickened with cold water)
apple slices

Bring all ingredients except apples to boil. Put apple slices in crust and pour juice over apples. Top with crust. Bake at 400° for one hour or until done.

Laura V. Troyer

AMISH WISDOM

Some beauty we can see,
some we can hear.
But the best we can feel inside.

***

After all, nature works sensibly,
for the fatter you get,
the further you must sit from the table.

PEACH CREAM PIE

1 tbsp. gelatin
1/4 c. cold water
3 c. fresh peaches

3/4 c. sugar
1/8 tsp. salt
1/2 c. cream (whipped)

Heat gelatin and water over hot water to dissolve gelatin. Slice peaches and add sugar. Let stand 10 minutes. Add dissolved gelatin and salt to peaches. Fold in whipped cream. Pour into baked pie shell. Chill 2 hours or more.

Barbara Miller

PINEAPPLE CREAM PIE

1 can Eagle Brand milk
3 tbsp. lemon juice
1 lg. Cool Whip

1 lg. can crushed pineapple
(drained)

Beat milk and lemon juice together. Then add pineapple and Cool Whip. Stir until well mixed. Pour into 2 graham cracker crusts. Chill several hours. Makes two 8 in. pies.

Mrs. Barbara Miller

STRAWBERRY PIE

1 pie shell, baked
1 8 oz. pkg. cream cheese
2 pints strawberries

1 c. sugar
3 tbsp. cornstarch - mixed
   with small amount of water

Soften and beat cream cheese until smooth. Spread evenly over baked pie shell. Slice 1 pint of strawberries and spread over cream cheese. Crush remaining pint of strawberries and bring to a boil. Add sugar and cornstarch mixture. Cook on medium heat for 2 minutes. Cool and pour over raw strawberries. Serve with whipped cream.

Lucie Byler

CUSTARD PIE

3 eggs, separated
1-1/2 c. sugar
1/4 tsp. salt
1 tsp. vanilla

1-3/4 c. milk
(1/2 evaporated;
1/2 regular)
cinnamon

Beat egg whites until stiff, then add yolks and beat a little more. Add the rest of the ingredients and mix well. Sprinkle cinnamon on top and bake in 400° oven for 15 to 20 minutes. Then reduce temperature to 350° and bake until firm. Done when inserted knife comes out clean.

Mrs. E. F. Miller

HERSHEY BAR PIE
(Candy Bar Pie)

17 marshmallows
1/4 lb. butter
6 Hershey bars with or
    without almonds

1/2 pint whipped cream
1 graham cracker crust

Melt marshmallows in top of double boiler with butter. Add Hershey bars. Melt all together and stir well. Cool mixture slightly and add whipped cream. Pour into graham cracker crust and chill before serving.

Ella M. Byler

COOKING HINT

Butter your pie pans lightly with butter.
It will help the pie crust to brown nicely.

LEMON PIE

3/4 c. sugar
3 tbsp. cornstarch
pinch of salt
2 c. cold water
2 egg yolks, beaten

juice of one lemon
1 tbsp. butter
1 tbsp. grated lemon rind
2 egg whites
1 9 in baked pie crust

Mix sugar, cornstarch, and salt. Slowly add water. Cook until thick. Add beaten egg yolks. Cool one minute. Add juice of lemon, butter and grated lemon rind. Cool. Beat egg whites until stiff. Add sugar to taste and whip until mixed. Pour lemon mixture into baked pie shell, top with meringue and put in 375° oven to brown lightly. Egg whites can be folded into lemon mixture for chiffon pie if desired.

AMISH VANILLA PIE

1 c. brown sugar
1 c. light Karo
2 tbsp. flour

1 beaten egg
2 c. water
2 tsp. vanilla

Combine in saucepan and boil until thickened. Mix together:

2 c. flour
1 tsp. soda
1 tsp. baking powder

1 c. brown sugar
1/2 c. shortening

Put liquid in bottom of pie crust and crumbs on top. Bake at 350°. Makes 2 pies.

Mrs. Owen Schmucker

LEMON SPONGE PIE

1 c. sugar
1 tbsp. butter
2 eggs
3 tbsp. flour

1 c. milk
1 lemon rind and juice
2 egg whites - beaten stiff

Mix sugar, butter, eggs and flour together. Add lemon and milk and then add stiffly-beaten egg whites. Pour into pie crusts and bake at 350° until done, about 25 minutes.

Sovilla Miller

LEMON CLOUD PIE

3/4 c. sugar
1/4 c. cornstarch
1 c. water
1 tsp. lemon rind-grated
1/3 c. lemon juice

2 egg yolks - slightly beaten
1/2 c. cream cheese
2 egg whites - beaten until
    until fluffy
1/4 c. sugar

Combine sugar, cornstarch, water, lemon rind, lemon juice and beaten egg yolks in a saucepan. Cook over medium heat until thick, stirring constantly. Remove from heat. Add cream cheese and blend well. Cool. Beat egg whites until stiff peaks form. Fold into lemon mixture. Pour into baked pie shell. Chill at least two hours.

Mrs. Melvin C. Miller

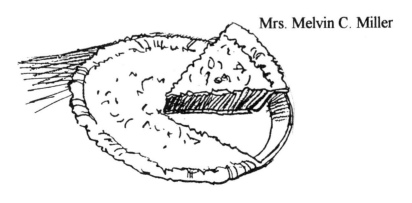

PEACH PECAN PIE

3 egg whites
1 c. sugar
24 squares soda crackers
1/4 tsp. baking powder

1/2 c. finely chopped nuts
1 tsp. vanilla
5-6 sliced peaches
1 pkg. Dream Whip

Beat egg whites until stiff, add sugar. Roll crackers until fine, mix with eggs, sugar, baking powder, nuts and vanilla. Pat mixture into a 9 in. buttered pan. Bake at 325° for 30 minutes. Let cool.

Filling:
Mix peaches with Dream Whip. Fill crust and refrigerate overnight.

Mrs. Susan Weaver

RAISIN CRUMB PIE

1/2 c. raisins
2 c. water
1 c. brown sugar

1 tbsp. vinegar
2 tbsp. cornstarch
pinch of salt

Place all ingredients in a saucepan except for cornstarch, which is used for thickening. Bring to boil. Thicken and cool. Pour into unbaked pie shell.

Crumbs:
1 c. flour
1/2 c. brown sugar

1/4 c. shortening
1/2 tsp. soda

Mix and put on top of raisin filling. Bake at 375° until shell is firm.

Mrs. Raymond M. Miller

COOKIE PIE CRUST

1 c. flour   2 tbsp. sugar
1 stick butter

Press in pie pan and bake at 400° until brown.

CREAM CHEESE FROSTING

2 3 oz. pkgs. cream cheese   1 tsp. vanilla
1/2 lb. powdered sugar   milk as needed

Combine ingredients, add just enough milk for spreading
consistency. Add nuts if desired.

BUTTER CRUNCH CRUST

1/2 c. margarine   1/4 c. brown sugar
1 c. flour   1/2 c. chopped nuts or
                                  shredded coconut

Mix together and spread in greased cookie sheet. Bake at 425°.
Take from oven and stir. Spread in pie pan. Cool and put in
favorite pudding mixture. Save crust for topping if you wish.

Mrs. Robert W. Detweiler

MILLIONAIRE PIE

1 c. powdered sugar   1/2 c. heavy whipping cream
1/4 c. margarine   1/4 c. chopped walnuts
1 small egg   1/2 c. drained crushed
1/8 tsp. salt   pineapple
1/8 tsp. vanilla

(continued next page)

Cream powdered sugar and margarine together. Add egg, salt, and vanilla and beat well. Spread the first mixture evenly over the bottom of a baked 8 in. pie shell. Chill. Whip heavy cream and fold in chopped nuts and crushed pineapple. Pile the whipping cream, pineapple, and nuts mixture on the top of the chilled filling in the pie shell. Chill until ready to serve. (The whipped cream is not sweetened - the bottom layer of the pie is sweetened enough so the unsweetened whipped cream is the perfect contrast.)

Mrs. E. F. Miller

OATMEAL PIE

3 eggs - beaten	2/3 c. oatmeal
2/3 c. white sugar	2/3 c. coconut
1 c. brown sugar	2/3 c. water
2 tsp. margarine	1 tsp. vanilla

Blend together and pour into unbaked pie shell. Bake for 30-35 minutes at 350°.

Mrs. Andy B. A. Byler

RHUBARB SPONGE PIE

1 c. sugar	2 eggs
1 tsp. butter	1 c. milk
2 tbsp. flour	1 c. rhubarb - cooked

Cream sugar and butter. Add flour and egg yolks and mix well. Add milk and rhubarb. Fold in beaten egg whites. Pour in unbaked pie shell and bake in 425° oven until done.

Mrs. Harvey W. Byler

FIVE PUMPKIN PIES

5 tbsp. flour - rounded
2 c. brown sugar
2 c. white sugar
1 large can pumpkin

12 eggs - beaten
2 qts. milk
3 tsp. pumpkin pie spice
1/2 tsp. salt

Mix ingredients together and pour into five unbaked pie shells.
Bake at 400° until done or until a knife inserted in middle comes
out clean.

Barbara Weaver

PUMPKIN PIE

3/4 c. canned pumpkin
1/2 c. brown sugar
1/2 c. white sugar
1 tbsp. flour
1/4 tsp. salt

1 tsp. cinnamon
1/4 tsp. pumpkin pie spice
2 c. milk
2 egg yolks

Mix together; then add 2 stiffly-beaten egg whites and beat
together with egg beater. Makes 2 small pies.

Mrs. Allen Detweiler

PIE CRUST

3 c. flour
1 tsp. salt
1-1/2 cup Crisco

1 egg
1 tbsp. vinegar
5 tbsp. cold water

Mix flour, salt and Crisco until it looks like peas. Beat egg and
vinegar and water. Add to flour. Mix well, chill and roll.

Mrs. Dan T. Yoder

HALF MOON PIES

1 gal. dried apple Snitz*   1 tbsp. allspice
6 c. water   1-1/2 tsp. cinnamon
6 c. sugar

Wash the Snitz and add the water. Cover and cook until soft and water is completely absorbed. Add sugar and cook 10 minutes longer. Remove from heat. Stir until smooth. Put through ricer. Set aside to cool. Make a pie dough, shaping the dough to the size of a walnut. Roll out dough balls into round pieces. Mark half of the dough with a pie crimper and on the other half place one large tablespoon of filling. Shape it like a half moon. Press edges together. Cut off remaining dough with pie crimper. Bake in hot (400°) oven. Makes 4 to 5 dozen.

Mrs. Herman Yoder

* Recipe for Snitz can be found in Table of Contents.

FRESH STRAWBERRY PIE

2 c. milk   1/2 c. sugar
3 tbsp. cornstarch   1 egg
pinch of salt   vanilla
1 pkg. Danish dessert   whipped cream
   (strawberry)

Cook together milk, sugar, cornstarch and egg. When cool, add one or two cups whipped cream. Pour into pie crust. Cook one package Danish dessert and mix in fresh strawberries. Pour on top of cornstarch pudding and top with Cool Whip. Makes two pies.

Mrs. John E. Miller

TABLE RULES

In silence I must take my seat,
and give God thanks before I eat.
Must for my food, in patience wait,
till I am asked to hand my plate.

I must not scold, nor whine nor pout,
nor move my chair or plate about.
With knife or fork or napkin ring,
I must not play nor must I sing.

I must not speak a useless word,
For children must be seen, not heard,
I must not talk about my food,
nor fret if I don't think it's good.

I must not say, "The bread is old",
"The tea is hot", "The coffee cold".
I must not cry for this or that,
nor murmur if my meat is fat.

My mouth with food, I must not crowd,
nor while I'm eating, speak aloud.
Must turn my head to cough or sneeze,
and when I ask, say "If you please."

The tablecloth, I must not spoil,
nor with my food, my fingers soil.
Must keep my seat till I am done,
nor round the table, sport and run.

When told to rise, then I must put
my chair away with noiseless foot.
And lift my heart to God above,
in praise for all His wondrous love.

An Amish friend

CHOCOLATE CREAM PIE

1-1/2 sticks margarine	4 eggs
3 squares chocolate	1 c. sugar
(pre-melted)	2 tsp. vanilla

Cream sugar and margarine. Add melted chocolate, vanilla, and eggs. Beat together with beater. Pour into graham cracker or butter crunch crust.

Mrs. John E. Miller

SUNSHINE PIE

A pound of patience, you must find,
mixed well with loving words, so kind.
Drop in two pounds of helpful deeds
and thoughts of other people's needs.

A pack of smiles, to make the crust,
then stir and bake it well you must.
And now, I ask that you may try,
the recipe of this Sunshine Pie.

Mrs. Jonas V. Miller

90

CREAM PUFFS

1 c. flour	1 c. water
1/4 tsp. salt	4 eggs
1/2 c. shortening	

Spoon unsifted flour into dry measuring cup. Level off and pour measured flour onto wax paper. Add salt to flour. Stir to blend. Bring shortening and water to boil in saucepan over medium heat. Add blended dry ingredients quickly. Beat constantly until mixture leaves sides of pan and forms a ball (about 1 minutes). Remove mixture from heat and cool slightly. Add eggs one at a time beating until smooth after each addition. Drop by heaping tablespoons onto ungreased baking sheets and bake at 400° for 40-45 minutes. Cool thoroughly and remove tops. Fill with cream filling and replace tops. Serve with frosting on top.

Cream Filling:

2. c. milk	5 tbsp. flour
2/3 c. sugar	1/4 tsp. salt
3 eggs, separated	1 tsp. vanilla

Scald 1-1/2 cup milk in top of double boiler. Combine sugar, flour and salt. Add remaining milk to dry ingredients to make smooth paste. Add paste to scalded milk and cook until thickened, stirring constantly. Slowly add beaten egg yolks and cook two more minutes. Remove from heat and add vanilla. Cool. When cooled add stiffly-beaten egg whites and blend into mixture.

Anna Marie Weaver

SNITZ FOR MOON PIES

1 gal. dried apples	1 tbsp. cinnamon
5 c. sugar	1/2 tsp. salt

Cook dried apples until soft. Put through a ricer and add cinnamon and mix. Makes 3-1/4 qt. prepared snitz.

Mary Miller

Cookies and Candies

NOTES ON FAVORITE RECIPES

BUTTERSCOTCH BARS

1/2 c. butter
2 c. brown sugar
2 eggs
1 tsp. vanilla
1 tsp. salt

2 c. flour
2 tsp. baking powder
1 c. coconut
1 c. nuts

Combine butter and brown sugar in a saucepan. Cook over low heat until hot and bubbly. Cool. Add eggs and beat well. Mix in dry ingredients and bake at 350° for 20-25 minutes.

Mrs. Freeman Miller

BROWNIES

1/2 c. flour
1/8 tsp. baking powder
1/8 tsp. salt
1/2 c. butter
1 c. nuts (chopped)

1 c. sugar
2 eggs
2 chocolate squares
 (melted)
1/2 tsp. vanilla

Cream sugar and butter, add eggs. Beat until light and fluffy. Beat in chocolate and vanilla. Add flour, baking powder, salt and nuts. Pour into lightly greased 8x8x2 inch pan. Bake at 350° for 30 minutes. Makes 16.

Mrs. John E. Miller

MYSTERY SQUARES

1/2 c. butter or margarine	1/2 c. coconut
1 c. flour	2 tbsp. flour
2 tbsp. white sugar	1/2 c. chopped walnuts
1-1/2 c. brown sugar	1 tsp. baking powder
2 eggs	

Mix butter, flour and white sugar. Spread evenly in bottom of square cake pan. Mix remaining ingredients and spread over first mixture. Bake at 350° for 45 min. or until done. Let cool in pan, then cut n small squares. Yield: 2 dozen bars.

Ada J. Shrock

FROSTED RAISIN BARS

1 c. raisins	1 tsp. cinnamon
1 c. water	1 tsp. cloves
1 c. sugar	1 tsp. nutmeg
1/3 c. shortening (oleo)	

Combine ingredients in saucepan and bring to a boil; let boil 5 minutes. Cool. Add:

2 c. flour	1/2 tsp. baking powder
3/4 tsp. soda	dash of salt

Mix together and spread in 10x15 in. pan. Bake 25 min. at 350°. When cool, frost with icing made with 1 c. powdered sugar, 2 tbsp. butter, 1/2 tsp. vanilla and enough milk to make spreading consistency.

Mrs. Barbara Miller

EASY TIME HOLIDAY SQUARES

1-1/2 c. sugar
1 c. butter
4 eggs
pie filling of choice

2 c. flour
1 tbsp. lemon extract
or juice

Cream sugar and shortening together. Add flour and lemon extract. Beat well. Pour batter into greased jelly roll pan. Mark off 24 squares. Place 1 heaping tbsp. of pie filling in center of each square. Bake about 40 min. at 350°. While warm, sift powdered sugar over top.

Esther Schmucker

HELLO DOLLIES - A BAR COOKIE

1 stick margarine
1-1/2 c. graham cracker
    crumbs
1-1/2 c. coconut

1 c. chocolate chips
1 c. nuts
1 c. sweetened condensed
    milk

Melt margarine in a 9x13 inch pan. Sprinkle on crumbs, coconut, chocolate chips and nuts. Pour condensed milk over top. Bake in 350° oven for 30 minutes. Cool and cut into squares.

Edna Mullet

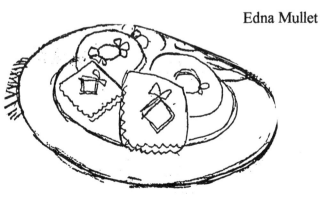

FUDGE NUT BARS

Cookie dough:

1 c. butter	1 tsp. baking soda
2 c. light brown sugar	1 tsp. salt
2 eggs	2-1/2 c. flour
2 tsp. vanilla	3 c. quick rolled oats

Mix and place in baking pan 13x9x2. Set aside.

Fudge Nut Filling:

1 12 oz. pkg. chocolate chips	1/2 tsp. salt
	1 c. chopped nuts
1 c. sweetened condensed milk	2 tsp. vanilla
	2 tbsp. butter

In sauce pan, over boiling water, mix chocolate chips, milk, butter and salt. Stir until chocolate chips are melted. Remove from heat and stir in chopped nuts and vanilla. Spread over cookie dough and bake at 350° for 25 to 30 minutes.

Mrs. Robert W. Detweiler

COCONUT COOKIES

1-1/2 c. sugar	2 eggs
1-1/2 c. brown sugar	1/4 c. water
1-1/2 c. shortening	1 tsp. soda
2 c. coconut	1 tsp. vanilla
4 c. flour	

Cream sugars and shortening. Add eggs and mix well. Add dry ingredients, water and vanilla. Add enough flour to make a fairly stiff batter. Stir in coconut. Drop by teaspoonfuls on cookie sheet. Bake at 375° for about 10 minutes.

Mrs. Lester Detweiler

WORLD'S BEST SUGAR COOKIES

1 c. powdered sugar	1 c. cooking oil
1 c. white sugar	1 tsp. salt
1 c. butter	1 tsp. baking soda
2 eggs	5 c. flour
2 tsp. vanilla	1 tsp. cream of tartar

Mix and roll into balls; press with a glass dipped in white sugar.
Bake at 350° for 15 minutes on an ungreased cookie sheet.

Mrs. John R. Schmucker

AUNT BETTY'S COOKIES

4 eggs	2 tsp. vanilla
2-2/3 c. brown sugar	4 tsp. cream of tartar
1-1/2 c. butter or lard	2 tsp. soda
6 c. flour	

Cream shortening and sugar; add vanilla and dry ingredients.
Make into a roll and let stand overnight. Next morning slice and
bake at 375° for 8-10 minutes.

CHOCOLATE CHIP COOKIES

1-1/2 c. white sugar	4 c. flour
1-1/2 c. brown sugar	1-1/2 c. shortening
2 eggs	1/2 tsp. salt
2 tbsp. water	1 tsp. vanilla
1 tsp. soda	2 c. chocolate chips

Cream sugar and shortening. Add eggs. Mix in dry ingredients
and add enough flour to form a very stiff batter. Add chips and
nuts. Drop by teaspoonfuls on cookie sheet 2 or 3 inches apart.
Bake at 375° for 10 minutes.

RANGER JOE COOKIES

1 c. shortening	1/2 tsp. baking powder
1 c. white sugar	2 c. flour
1 c. brown sugar	2 c. Rice Krispies
2 eggs	2 c. oatmeal
1 tsp. vanilla	1 c. coconut
1/2 c. chocolate chips	1/2 tsp. salt
1 tsp. soda	1/2 c. walnuts

Mix in order given. Roll into small balls and flatten with fork. Bake on greased cookie sheets at 375° for 9-11 minutes.

Mrs. Ervin E. Miller

COCOA CHEESE SANDWICH COOKIES

2 c. all purpose flour	3/4 c. butter
1/2 tsp. salt	1 egg
3/4 c. sugar	1 tsp. vanilla
1/3 c. cocoa	pecan halves

In a large bowl, combine all ingredients except pecans and filling. Blend well at low speed. Divide dough in half; shape into two 2 inch rolls. Wrap in wax paper; chill at least 2 hours. Cut into slices about 1/8 inch thick; place on ungreased cookie sheets. Garnish half the slices (for cookie tops) with a pecan half. Bake at 350° for 8 to 10 minutes. Place 2 cookies together with the following filling in the middle, sandwich style, using a plain slice for the bottom half.

Cheese Filling:

3 tbsp. butter	2 c. confectioners sugar
1 tbsp. cream	1/4 tsp. salt
3 oz. pkg. cream cheese, softened	

Blend all ingredients together until creamy and smooth.

SALTED PEANUT CRISPS

1 c. butter
1-1/2 c. brown sugar
  packed
2 eggs
2 tsp. vanilla

3 c. flour
1/2 tsp. soda
1 tsp. salt
2 c. salted peanuts

Mix butter, sugar, eggs and vanilla. Blend flour, soda and salt; stir into creamed mixture. Add peanuts. Drop by rounded teaspoons on a lightly greased cookie sheet. Flatten with bottom of greased glass dipped in sugar. Bake for 8-10 minutes or until golden brown in 375° oven. Makes about 6 dozen 2-inch cookies. Note: If you use Gold Medal self-rising flour, omit soda and salt.

Barbara Weaver

MOLASSES NUT COOKIES

6 c. flour
3 tsp. baking soda
3 tsp. cinnamon
2 tsp. ginger
1 tsp. salt
2 1/2 c. sugar

1 c. molasses
2 c. sour milk
1 tsp. vanilla
1 c. chopped nuts
1 c. shortening

Cream sugar and shortening. Add eggs, molasses and vanilla. Mix dry ingredients together and add alternately with sour milk to creamed mixture. Stir in nuts. Drop on greased cookie sheet by teaspoonfuls and bake at 375° for 9-11 minutes.

Mrs. Ray D. Byler

FANNIE'S CHIP COOKIES

1 c. butter	3-3/4 c. flour
1 c. white sugar	1 tsp. soda
1-1/2 c. brown sugar	1 tsp. vanilla
4 eggs	1 lg. pkg. chocolate chips

Cream sugars, shortening, vanilla and eggs. Add dry ingredients, mix well and add 1 pkg. chocolate chips and 1 c. nuts (optional). Drop by teaspoonfuls on ungreased cookie sheet. Bake at 350° about ten minutes.

Susan Gingerich

GINGER CREAMS

1 c. sugar	1 tsp. cloves
1/2 c. shortening	1 tsp. cinnamon
2 eggs well beaten	1 tsp. ginger
1 c. cold water	4 c. flour
1 c. baking molasses	1 tsp. salt
1 tsp. soda	1 c. chopped nuts
1 tsp. nutmeg	

Cream shortening and sugar. Add beaten eggs, molasses and water. Beat well. Add dry ingredients and mix well. Drop by spoonfuls onto greased baking sheet. Bake at 375° 10-12 minutes. Frost when cool.

Icing:

6 tbsp. butter	1 tsp. vanilla
3 tbsp. hot water	confectioners sugar

Melt butter, add hot water and vanilla. Thicken with confectioners sugar. Beat until a creamy consistency.

Saloma Hershberger

GRAHAM GEMS

1 c. graham flour	3 tbsp. shortening
1 c. white flour	3/4 tsp. salt
1 c. milk	4 tsp. baking powder
2 tbsp. molasses or sugar	1 egg

Mix dry ingredients, add milk, egg, melted shortening and molasses (or sugar). Mix well. Spoon into muffin tins half full. Bake at 400° for 25 minutes.

Emma Beachey

NO BAKE OATMEAL COOKIES

1/2 lb. butter	2 c. white sugar
1/2 c. milk	2 tsp. vanilla
4 tbsp. peanut butter	4 c. oatmeal

Bring to a rolling boil, stirring often. Then add oatmeal; drop on waxed paper. Let set until cool.

Mrs. Andy B. A. Byler

SOFT MAPLE COOKIES

1 c. brown sugar	1-1/2 tsp. baking powder
3/4 c. margarine	1/2 tsp. soda
1 egg	1 tsp. salt
3/4 c. milk	1 tsp. vanilla
3 c. flour	1 tsp. maple flavoring

Mix shortening and sugar. Add egg and milk. Add remaining ingredients. Beat thoroughly. Drop by teaspoonfuls on greased cookie sheet. Bake at 375° for 10 minutes.
(continued)

Icing:

| 1 c. powdered sugar | 1 tsp. vanilla |
| 1 tbsp. Crisco | 3 tbsp. milk |

Lydia Troyer

RAISIN PUFFS

1-1/2 c. raisins   1 c. water

Boil raisins in water until all the water is absorbed. Cool and set aside.

1 c. margarine	1 tsp. soda
1-1/2 c. sugar	3 eggs
1 tsp. vanilla	3-1/2 c. flour

Cream sugar and shortening. Add eggs. Add dry ingredients and vanilla. Mix well. Add raisins and refrigerate for a few hours. Roll into balls the size of a walnut and roll in sugar. Place on a greased cookie sheet and bake at 350° until very light brown.

Anna Marie Weaver

AMISH WISDOM

If there's not enough to save,
but a little too much to dump,
and you just can't help but eat it,
that's what makes the housewife plump!

******

101

DELICIOUS CHERRY BARS

1 c. nuts	8 oz. cream cheese
1-1/4 c. flour	1/3 c. milk
1/2 c. brown sugar	1 egg
1/2 c. butter	1 tsp. vanilla
1/2 c. coconut	1 can cherry pie filling

Combine flour, brown sugar and butter and blend to fine crumbs. Add coconut and 1/2 c. nuts. Set aside 1/2 c. crumbs and pack the rest into 9x13 in. greased baking dish. Bake at 350° for 15 minutes.

Soften cream cheese and add sugar, egg and vanilla. Spread over hot baked layer and bake 10 minutes.

Spread cherry pie filling over top and sprinkle with remaining nuts and reserved crumbs. Bake 15 minutes longer.

Mrs. Freeman Miller

CHOCOLATE CHIP BARS

2 c. flour	4 eggs
2 c. sugar	1-1/2 tsp. salt
2 tsp. baking powder	1/2 c. butter
2 c. chocolate chips	1 tsp. vanilla

Mix together; then spread on cookie sheet. Bake 25 minutes in 350° oven. Don't over bake. When cool, cut into bars.

Emma Beachey

SOFT WHITE DROP COOKIES

1-1/4 c. sugar
1-1/4 c. brown sugar
2 eggs
1-1/2 c. milk
1 c. Wesson oil
(add last)

1 tsp. vanilla
3 tsp. soda
1-1/2 tsp. salt
5 c. flour
2 c. powdered sugar*

(* Do not mix with other ingredients)

Cream sugars and eggs, add vanilla. Add dry ingredients and milk alternately. Add Wesson oil. Drop by spoonfuls on cookie sheet. Bake at 375° until done. Let cookies cool slightly and roll in powdered sugar.

Mrs. William W. Hochstetler

CHOCOLATE MARSHMALLOW COOKIES

1 c. brown sugar
1 egg
1 tsp. vanilla
1/2 tsp. soda
1/2 c. cocoa
1/2 c. shortening

1/2 c. milk
1-3/4 c. sifted flour
1/2 tsp. salt
1/2 c. chopped nuts
marshmallows
powdered sugar

Cream sugar and shortening; add egg. Add dry ingredients alternately with milk. Add nuts and mix well. Drop by spoonfuls onto cookie sheets. Bake at 350° for 8 minutes. After baking, top with 1/2 of the marshmallows and return to oven until marshmallow is warm. Sprinkle with powdered sugar.

Mrs. Susan Weaver

BUTTERSCOTCH BIT COOKIES

3 c. brown sugar
2 c. white sugar
2-1/2 c. lard or butter
   melted
3 c. milk

1 pkg. butterscotch bits
6 tsp. baking powder
3 tsp. baking soda
4 eggs
1 tbsp. vanilla

Cream lard and sugar. Add beaten eggs; beat well. Add milk,
beat in flour, baking powder, baking soda and vanilla. Beat well.
Then beat in butterscotch bits. Drop on cookie sheets and bake
at 350° until golden brown.

Liz Miller

BANANA NUT BARS

2-1/2 c. all-purpose flour
1-2/3 c. sugar
1-1/4 tsp. baking powder
1-1/4 tsp. baking soda
1 tsp. salt
3/4 c. butter or oleo
   (softened)

2/3 c. buttermilk or sour
   milk
1-1/4 c. very ripe mashed
   bananas
2 eggs
1/2 c. chopped nuts

In a three-quart bowl mix all dry ingredients. Add butter,
buttermilk and bananas. Beat until moistened, add eggs; beat 2
more minutes. Stir in nuts; turn into ungreased 10 in. pan. Bake
at 350° oven 30-40 minutes

Mrs. Barbara Miller

COOKING HINT

*Boiled frostings will not harden
if 3/4 tsp. vanilla is added while cooking*

OUT-OF-THIS-WORLD COOKIES

1 c. white sugar	1/2 c. crushed corn flakes
1 c. peanut butter	1 c. finely chopped nuts
1 c. finely chopped dates	1 lg. bag chocolate chips, melted, or dipping choc.

Cream sugar and peanut butter. Add dates, nuts and corn flakes. Mix well, then shape into balls. Let mixture sit overnight. Dip into chocolate and chill until mixture hardens.

LAZY SUGAR COOKIES

1/3 c. butter	1/2 c. shortening
1/2 c. sugar	1/2 c. powdered sugar
1-1/2 tsp. vanilla	1 egg
1/2 tsp. cream of tartar	1/2 tsp. soda
1/2 tsp. salt	2-1/4 c. flour

Cream shortening and sugar together. Add vanilla, egg, cream of tartar, soda and salt. Mix well. Add flour and mix well. Roll dough in balls, flatten with glass dipped in sugar. Bake in 350° oven for 10-12 minutes.

Mrs. John E. Miller

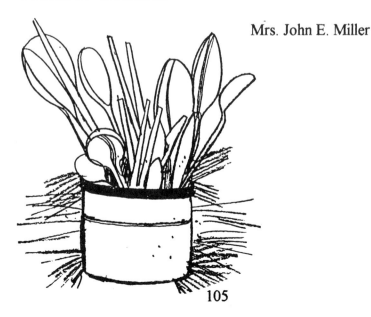

MAPLE SANDWICH COOKIES

1/2 c. butter	1 tsp. soda
1 c. brown sugar	1/2 tsp. salt
2 eggs	2 tbsp. cream
1 tbsp. maple flavor	2-3/4 c. flour

Mix together in order given, chill a few hours. Roll out and cut in size of sandwich cookies. Bake at 400° for 10-12 minutes. Cool. When cold put 2 cookies together with frosting as follows:

Frosting:

2 beaten egg whites	2 c. confectioners sugar
1 tsp. maple flavor	1-1/2 c. soft butter

Beat egg whites stiff, add flavor and sugar; beat until smooth. Add butter and continue to beat or stir until well mixed.

Elizabeth Miller

SUGAR COOKIES

1 c. melted margarine	1/4 tsp. salt
2 c. sugar	1 tsp. vanilla
2 eggs	1 c. milk
2 tsp. soda	5 c. flour
4 tsp. baking powder	

Mix shortening, sugar and eggs and beat. Add soda, baking powder, salt and vanilla, beat again. Then add milk and flour alternately. Bake in hot oven at 475° for approximately 15 minutes.

Kathryn Hostetler

TOLL HOUSE COOKIES

2-1/2 c. brown sugar
2-1/2 c. white sugar
4 c. shortening
8 eggs
1 tbsp. hot water

4 tsp. soda
10 c. flour
5 c. chocolate chips
4 c. nuts
vanilla - salt

Mix together in order given, drop on greased sheet and bake at 375° for 10-12 minutes.

Elizabeth Miller

DROP GINGER COOKIES

1 c. sugar
1 c. molasses
1 c. shortening
2 eggs

1 tsp. soda
1 c. sour milk
4 c. flour
1 tsp. ginger

Cream sugar, shortening, eggs and molasses together. Add in dry ingredients and sour milk alternately. Drop by teaspoonfuls on cookie sheet and bake at 350° for 8-10 minutes.

Mrs. Ray D. Byler

SPICY HONEY COOKIES

1 c. sugar
1/2 c. shortening
1 egg
1/4 c. honey
2-1/2 c. flour
1 tsp. cinnamon

2 tbsp. milk
1 tsp. vanilla
2 tsp. soda
3/4 tsp. salt
3/4 tsp. nutmeg

Cream sugar, shortening, egg and honey. Add dry ingredients and milk. Mix well.

Form dough into small balls. Dip one side in 3 tbsp. milk and then in sugar. Place on cookie sheet, sugar side up. Bake at 350° for 12-15 minutes.

OATMEAL SUGAR COOKIES

1 c. shortening
1 c. sugar
1 c. brown sugar
3 eggs
4 tsp. vinegar
2 tsp. vanilla
nuts if desired

1/3 c. milk
2 c. oatmeal
4 c. flour
1 tsp. salt
1-1/2 tsp. soda
6 oz. pkg. chocolate chips

Cream shortening, brown sugar and white sugar. Add eggs, vinegar and vanilla, mix well. Stir in dry ingredients and mix thoroughly. Add chocolate chips and nuts. Drop by teaspoonfuls on ungreased baking sheet. Bake at 375° 9-11 minutes.

Mrs. Robert W. Detweiler

RAISIN PUFFS

1-1/2 c. raisins	1 tsp. salt
1-1/2 c. shortening	3-1/2 c. flour
1-1/2 c. sugar	1 tsp. soda
3 eggs	1 tsp. vanilla

Boil raisins in one cup water until water is gone. Cool.
Combine other ingredients, putting raisins in last. Roll in balls
and then roll in sugar. Bake at 350° until lightly browned.

Laura V. Troyer

COCONUT OATMEAL COOKIES

2 c. shortening	4 c. flour
2 c. white sugar	2 tsp. soda
2 c. brown sugar	2 tsp. baking powder
4 eggs, beaten	1 tsp. vanilla
5 c. rolled oats	1 c. nuts
2 c. coconut	1 pkg. chocolate chips

Sift flour, salt, baking powder and soda. Cream sugars and
shortening. Add beaten eggs, vanilla and coconut. Stir in dry
ingredients and rolled oats. Chill dough; form into balls the size
of a walnut. Place 2 inches apart on a cookie sheet. Bake at
375° until done; about 10-12 minutes.

Mrs. Freeman Miller

SOFT CHOCOLATE CHIP COOKIES

1 c. melted butter	3-1/2 c. flour
2 c. brown sugar	1 tsp. soda
2 eggs	1 tsp. soda
1/2 c. sour milk	1 small bag chocolate
1 tsp. vanilla	chips

Cream sugar and shortening; add eggs, mix well. Add vanilla and mix in dry ingredients and chocolate chips. Drop by spoonfuls on ungreased cookie sheet. Bake at 375° for 10 minutes.

Mrs. Allen Detweiler

CHOCOLATE CRUNCH

1/2 c. butter (melted)	3 tsp. vanilla
1/2 c. light Karo syrup	4 c. quick rolled oats
1 c. brown sugar	1-1/2 c. chocolate chips
1 tsp. salt	2 c. miniature marshmallows

Mix butter, Karo, sugar, salt, vanilla and rolled oats and spread into a buttered pan with a damp spatula. Bake at 400° for 10 minutes. Remove from oven, sprinkle top with chocolate chips and marshmallows. Return to oven and bake for 3 more minutes.

Saloma Hershberger

COOKING HINT FOR CAKES

Use a knife dipped in water
for smoothing on icing. Goes on much easier.

MAPLE DROP COOKIES

1 c. brown sugar
1 c. butter
3 eggs
5 c. flour
1/2 tsp. salt
1 tsp. soda

1/2 c. milk
1 tsp. vanilla
1 tsp. maple flavoring
1 tsp. baking powder
1 c. nuts

Cream sugar, butter and eggs together. Add salt, soda, baking powder, vanilla and maple flavoring. Add milk and flour. Drop by teaspoonfuls on greased cookie sheet. Bake in 375° oven for 9-11 minutes or until done. Cool and frost.

Frosting:

1-1/2 c. powdered sugar
2 tbsp. shortening

Maple flavoring

Mix well. Add enough milk to make a spreading consistency.

Mrs. Ervin E. Miller

SUGAR AND SPICE SNAPS

3/4 c. melted butter
1 c. sugar
1 egg
1/4 c. honey

2-1/4 c. flour
2 tsp. soda
1/2 tsp. nutmeg

Cream butter, sugar and egg; add honey. Mix in dry ingredients and form into balls, roll in sugar and bake at 350° for 8-10 minutes.

BUTTERSCOTCH CHIP COOKIES

1 c. butter
2 c. brown sugar
2 eggs
1/2 c. sour milk
1 tsp. vanilla

3-1/2 c. flour
1 tsp. soda
1/2 tsp. salt
1 c. butterscotch chips
1/2 c. chopped nuts

Cream butter and sugar, add beaten eggs, sour milk and vanilla. Mix in flour, soda and salt. Add chips and nuts last. Bake on ungreased cookie sheets 12-15 min. at 350°.

Mrs. Emma Yoder

PUMPKIN CHOCOLATE CHIP COOKIES

1-1/2 c. sugar
1/2 c. softened butter
1 egg
2-1/2 c. flour
1 tsp. baking powder
1 tsp. baking soda
1 c. nuts

1 tsp. cinnamon
1/2 tsp. salt
1 c. cooked or canned
  pumpkin
1 tsp. vanilla
1 c. chocolate chips

Cream sugar and butter with egg. Sift dry ingredients together and add alternately to creamed mixture with pumpkin. Stir in vanilla, chocolate chips and nuts. Drop by teaspoonfuls on greased cookie sheet. Bake at 350° about 10-12 minutes.

Fannie D. Miller

RAISIN DROP COOKIES

1 c. water	1 tsp. baking powder
2 c. raisins	1 tsp. vanilla
1 tsp. baking soda	1/4 tsp. nutmeg
1 c. butter	1/4 tsp. salt
2 c. sugar	3-1/3 c. flour
3 eggs	

Cook raisins and water for 5 minutes. Let cool and stir in baking soda; let stand. Cream sugar and butter; add eggs and vanilla. Add dry ingredients and raisins with juice. Mix well. Drop on a cookie sheet by teaspoon and bake at 400° for about 12-15 minutes.

Susan Gingerich

BUTTER BALLS

1/2 c. butter	1/2 c. finely chopped nuts
1/4 c. powdered sugar	1/2 tsp. vanilla
1-1/4 c. flour	

Cream butter and sugar, add flour, vanilla and nuts. Mix well. Roll into balls and bake at 350° for 15 minutes. Do not brown. Roll in powdered sugar while still warm.

Mrs. William W. Hochstetler

HUMOROUS AMISH SAYINGS

*A girl's shoe comin' untied,
or her stockin' comin' down,
means her boyfriend is thinkin' of her.*

MAPLE TOP MELTAWAYS

1 c. butter
1 c. sugar
1 tbsp. milk
1 tsp. vanilla
2 c. flour

1/2 c. nuts
1/2 c. semi-sweet
   chocolate chips
1/2 c. butterscotch chips

Cream butter and sugar together. Blend in milk and vanilla, add flour and nuts. Spread into ungreased 13x9x2 pan. Bake at 325° for 35 to 40 minutes until golden brown. Remove from oven and immediately sprinkle with chocolate and butterscotch chips. Let stand for 5 minutes. When chips have softened, spread to make frosting.

Mrs. William W. Hochstetler

CHOCOLATE NO BAKE COOKIES

2 c. white sugar
3 tbsp. cocoa
1/4 c. butter
1/2 c. milk

1/2 c. peanut butter
3 c. oatmeal
1 tsp. vanilla

Boil sugar, cocoa, butter and milk for one minute. Remove from heat. Add oatmeal (crumbled fine), vanilla and peanut butter. Drop quickly on waxed paper by teaspoonfuls. Coconut, nuts, chocolate chips may be used instead of peanut butter. Cool until firm.

COOKING HINT

After filling baking pans with batter,
tap sharply on counter to let air bubbles burst.

PEANUT BLOSSOMS

1-3/4 c. Pillsbury all-
   purpose flour
1/2 c. sugar
1/2 c. brown sugar -
   packed
1 tsp. soda
1/2 tsp. salt

1/2 c. shortening
1/2 c. peanut butter
1 egg
2 tbsp. milk
1 tsp. vanilla
48 milk chocolate kisses

Combine all ingredients in a large mixing bowl except chocolate kisses. Blend well at low speed. Shape into balls, using rounded teaspoonful for each. Roll balls in additional sugar. Place on ungreased cookie sheets. Bake at 375° for 10 - 12 minutes. Remove from oven. Top each cookie immediately with a candy kiss, pressing down firmly so cookie cracks around edge.

Barbara Weaver

WHOPPIE PIES

4 c. sifted flour
2 c. sugar
1 c. shortening
1 c. cocoa
2 tsp. soda

2 tsp. salt
2 tsp. vanilla
2 eggs
1 c. sour milk
1 c. hot water

Mix all together and drop by teaspoonfuls on cookie sheet. Bake at 400° for 8 to 10 minutes. Cool.

Filling or Frosting:
2 egg whites
3/4 c. butter
4 c. powdered sugar

4 tbsp. cream
2 tsp. vanilla

Mix all filling ingredients together and spread between two cookies to make a sandwich cookie called Whoppie Pies.

Mrs. Lester Detweiler

MOLASSES CRINKLES

4 c. soft shortening
1 c. brown sugar, packed
1 egg
1/4 c. molasses
2-1/4 c. Gold Medal flour

2 tsp. soda
1/4 tsp. salt
1/2 tsp. cloves
1 tsp. cinnamon
1 tsp. ginger

Mix shortening, sugar, eggs and molasses thoroughly. Sift flour and measure. Blend all dry ingredients, and mix with sugar - egg mixture. Stir and chill. Roll dough in 1-1/4 in. balls, dip tops in sugar and place sugared side up, 3 inches apart, on a greased cookie sheet. Sprinkle each with 2 or 3 drops of water. Bake in 375° oven for 10 to 12 minutes or just until set but not hard. Makes 4 dozen cookies.

Mrs. Joe J. Weaver

OATMEAL DROP COOKIES

1/2 c. shortening
1-1/2 c. sugar
2 eggs
1/3 c. molasses
1-3/4 c. Gold Medal Flour
1 tsp. soda

1 tsp. salt
1 tsp. cinnamon
2 c. rolled oats
1/2 c. chopped nuts
1 c. raisins

Mix shortening, sugar, eggs and molasses thoroughly. Measure flour. Stir dry ingredients together. Blend into creamed mixture. Stir in oats, nuts and raisins. Drop dough by rounded teaspoonfuls about 2 inches apart on lightly greased baking sheet. Bake 8 to 10 minutes or until lightly brown. Makes 6 dozen cookies.

Mrs. Joe J. Weaver

FROSTED CREAMS

1 c. baking molasses   1 tsp. cinnamon
1 tbsp. soda   1/2 c. water
1 c. sugar   3 egg yolks
1 tbsp. baking powder   5 c. flour (approx.)
1 c. butter

Mix all ingredients and drop by spoonfuls on a ungreased cookie sheet, bake at 350° for 8-9 minutes or until they feel done. Cool.

Frosting:
2 tbsp. Karo   4 tbsp. water
1-1/2 c. powdered sugar   2 egg whites, beaten

Boil Karo, sugar and water until threads appear when poured from fork. Pour mixture into beaten egg whites. Beat until smooth. Spread on cookies.

APPLE SQUARES

3 eggs   1 tsp. soda
1-3/4 c. sugar   1 tsp. cinnamon
1 c. corn oil   4 to 6 tart apples,
1/4 tsp. salt   sliced or 1 c.
2 c. flour   mashed bananas
1 c. nuts

Cream oil, sugar and eggs. Add dry ingredients and sliced apples and nuts. Bake on lightly greased cookie sheet at 350° for 25 to 30 minutes. (If you use mashed bananas instead of apples, increase flour 1/2 cup and add 1 tsp. of orange flavoring.)

Betty Shrock

MONSTER COOKIES

1 lb. butter	18 c. oatmeal
2 lb. brown sugar	1 lb. chocolate chips
(4 c. packed)	1 lb. M&M's candy pieces
4 c. white sugar	1/2 c. vanilla
1 dozen eggs	3 lb. peanut butter
2 c. nuts, chopped	8 tsp. soda

Combine first four ingredients and mix. Add remaining ingredients. Drop by teaspoonfuls onto cookie sheet. Bake at 350° for 10 minutes. Makes very large batch.

Mrs. Lester Detweiler

PUMPKIN COOKIES

1 c. lard	1 c. brown sugar
1 c. pumpkin	2 c. flour
1 tsp. cinnamon	1 tsp. soda
1 tsp. baking powder	1/2 tsp. salt
1 egg	

Mix together sugar, lard and egg. Add pumpkin. Add the other ingredients with dates and nuts. Drop by spoonfuls on greased cookie sheet. Bake at 375° for 10 to 12 minutes. Frost with orange icing.

Mrs. Herman Yoder

HOUSEHOLD HINT

Use soda in wash water for dishes.
It refreshes, removes stains and softens the water.

GRAHAM CRACKERS

2 c. sugar
4 c. sifted graham flour
1 tsp. soda
1 tsp. salt
1 tsp. vanilla

2 c. flour
1 c. shortening
1 tsp. baking powder
1 c. milk

Mix, roll thin, cut and prick with fork. Bake in 350° oven until nice and brown.

Katherine M. Byler

MOLASSES GINGER COOKIES

2 c. baking molasses
1 c. brown sugar
1/2 c. melted butter
1 c. melted lard
2/3 c. boiling water

4 tsp. soda
1 tbsp. ginger
1 tsp. cinnamon
1/4 tsp. salt
8 c. flour

Mix ingredients and drop by teaspoonfuls on cookie sheet. Bake at 375° about 10 minutes. Do not over bake.

Mrs. Elie Wengerd

SODA CRACKERS

7 c. flour
1 tsp. soda
1 tsp. baking powder

1-1/4 c. lard
1 tbsp. salt
1-1/2 c. cream or milk

Mix like pie dough with a fork or pastry blender. Roll out dough and cut in squares. Bake on cookie sheets at 350° until browned.

Katherine M. Byler

CHOCOLATE PEANUT CLUSTERS

1/2 lb. sweet chocolate
1 c. peanuts

2/3 c. Eagle Brand
sweetened condensed milk

Melt chocolate in top of double boiler over boiling water.
Remove from heat, add condensed milk and peanuts, mix well.
Drop by teaspoonfuls on waxed paper.

TURTLES

1 lb. brown sugar
1/2 lb. butter
1 can condensed milk

1 tsp. cream of tartar
1 c. Karo syrup

Mix all ingredients together in a pan. Boil for 12 minutes,
stirring constantly. Slightly cool. Spread cookie sheets with
pecans. Drop by tablespoonfuls of caramel on tops of pecans -
about an inch apart. When set, dip in melted chocolate.

Anna Marie Weaver

RAISIN FILLED COOKIES

1-1/2 c. white sugar
1-1/2 c. brown sugar
1 c. sweet milk
2 tsp. soda
2 tsp. vanilla

1 c. lard
3 eggs
3 tsp. baking powder
flour to roll

Cream sugars and shortening. Add eggs. Mix in dry ingredients and mix well. Chill dough. Roll to about 3/16 inch thick. Bake at 375° about 10 minutes. Use following filling between 2 cookies:

Filling:
2 c. raisins (ground)
1 c. water

1 c. sugar
1/2 c. nuts

Cook until thick. Cool.

Mrs. Eli Wengerd

PEANUT BUTTER PATTIES

2 lb. powdered sugar
6 c. Rice Krispies
4 c. crunchy peanut butter
pinch of salt

2 sticks butter
1 lg. pkg. chocolate chips
   or coating chocolate

Mix all ingredients together. Melt chocolate chips. Make candy into small patties and dip in chocolate; let set. Makes a large batch.

Mrs. Dan J. M. Miller

BUCKEYES

1 stick softened butter or
  margarine
1-1/2 c. peanut butter
1/2 cake paraffin

1 lb. powdered sugar
1 tsp. vanilla
1- 12oz. pkg. chocolate chips

Blend well. Roll into balls and chill several hours or overnight. Then dip in the following contents kept in a double boiler: One 12 oz. pkg. chocolate chips and 1/2 cake paraffin. Dip the balls into the melted chocolate mixture using a toothpick in the center of the peanut butter balls.

Mary Miller

BAKED CARAMEL CORN

2 sticks butter
2 c. packed brown sugar
1/2 c. white Karo

1 tsp. vanilla
1 tsp. soda
10-12 cups popped corn

Mix first three ingredients. Put on heat, stir until boiling. Cook 5 minutes without stirring. Take off heat and stir in vanilla and soda. Mix into a large pan of popped corn. Put in roaster and bake in a 250° oven for 1/2 hour. Stir often while baking.

Mrs. Emma Yoder

PEPPERMINT PATTIES

3 oz. cream cheese,
  softened
1/4 lb. butter
1/2 can sweet condensed milk
16 oz. coating chocolate or
  semi-sweet chocolate chips

2-1/2 lb. confectioner's
  sugar
1 tsp. peppermint
  flavoring

Mix all ingredients thoroughly and chill. Form small balls with a melon scoop or with your hands. Dip in melted chocolate and let set until firm.

Mrs. John R. Schmucker

PEANUT BUTTER CANDY BALLS

1 lb. confectioner's sugar
2 tsp. salt
melted milk chocolate
  (coating chocolate)

2 c. peanut butter
1 c. butter, melted

Mix and roll in balls and dip in melted milk chocolate.

Mrs. Elmer L. Yoder

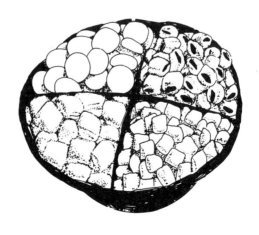

VANILLA FUDGE

6 c. white sugar	1 tsp. salt
3 c. cream	1 tsp. vanilla
1 c. white Karo	1/2 stick butter

Mix ingredients except vanilla and cook to 238° on candy thermometer or until small amount dripped into cold water forms a soft ball that flattens when removed from water. Cool without stirring to 120° or until bottom of pan is lukewarm. Add vanilla. Beat continuously with wooden spoon until candy is thick and no longer glossy, probably 5-10 minutes. Pour into buttered loaf pan, 9x5x3 and cool until firm. Cut into 1 inch squares.

Mrs. Andy B. A. Byler

CHOCOLATE FUDGE

1 c. sugar	1 tbsp. corn syrup
1/3 c. cocoa	1 tsp. vanilla
1/4 c. butter	1/2 c. chopped nuts
1/4 c. milk	2-1/2 to 3 c. confectioners sugar

Mix cocoa and sugar. Stir in butter, milk and corn syrup. Bring to a boil. Boil for 1 minute, stirring occasionally. Remove from heat. Add vanilla and chopped nuts immediately. Add confectioner's sugar 1 cup at a time. Turn into an ungreased square pan, 8x8x2 in., and pat with fingers. Cool. Cut into squares. Makes about 36 squares.

Mrs. Joe J. Weaver

PEANUT BUTTER CUPS

1 box powdered sugar	2 c. peanut butter
1 c. butter	2 Hershey bars
2 tsp. salt	(largest size)

Mix all ingredients but chocolate together into balls. Chill. Melt milk chocolate in a double boiler, then dip balls in chocolate. Place on waxed paper to set.

BUTTERMILK COOKIES

1 c. margarine	2 eggs
1 c. brown sugar	pinch of salt
1 c. white sugar	2 tsp. baking soda
4 c. flour	1 tsp. vanilla
1 c. buttermilk	

Cream margarine, sugar, eggs and vanilla. Add dry ingredients and buttermilk alternately and mix well. Chill 2 to 3 hours in refrigerator. Roll dough 1/4 inch thick on well floured cloth. Cut into circles. Place on greased cookie sheet 1-1/2 inches apart. Bake at 375° for 10-12 minutes. Cool.

Mrs. Elmer L. Yoder

AMISH POEM

Come, let's clean out the garden.
Carry in everything we find.
Stuff it all in, jars,
shapes of every kind.

When winter comes a howling,
along the shelves we'll snoop.
And serve our hungry family,
with some vegetables and soup.

AUNTIE MAE'S COOKIES

1 c. butter

2 eggs

1-1/2 c. sugar

4 tsp. baking powder

1 tsp. soda

1/4 tsp. salt

1 tsp. vanilla

1 c. milk

4 c. flour

Cream butter, sugar, eggs and vanilla. Add dry ingredients and mix thoroughly. Drop by teaspoonfuls on ungreased cookie sheet. Bake at 375° for 10 minutes. This cookie may be eaten plain, dusted with colored or powdered sugars or frosted. These cookies stay soft.

Mrs. Robert E. Detweiler

BUTTER PECAN COOKIES

1 c. butter

3/4 c. brown sugar

3/4 c. white sugar

2 eggs

1 c. pecans

2-1/4 c. flour

1 tsp. soda

1 tsp. vanilla

dash salt

Mix together and drop by teaspoonfuls on an ungreased cookie sheet. Bake at 375° until brown. Makes 4 dozen.

Fannie D. Miller

COOKING HINT
When boiling beets or potatoes,
put a little butter in the pot.
It will keep it from boiling over.

THREE-MINUTE FUDGE

2/3 c. evaporated milk
1-2/3 c. sugar
1/2 tsp. salt
2 c. marshmallows,
  miniature

1-1/2 c. semi-sweet
  chocolate chips
1 tsp. vanilla
1/2 c. chopped nuts

Mix milk, sugar and salt in a saucepan. Heat to boiling over low heat. Boil and stir for 3 minutes. Remove from heat. Add chocolate chips and marshmallows. Stir until both are melted. Pour into a buttered, square pan - 9x9x2 inches. Chill until firm. Cut into squares.

Kathryn Hostetler

PULL TAFFY

1 c. sugar
3/4 c. light corn syrup
2/3 c. water
1 tbsp. cornstarch

2 tbsp. butter
1 tsp. salt
2 tsp. vanilla

Mix sugar, corn syrup, water, cornstarch, butter and salt. Heat to boiling over medium heat. Stir constantly. Cook without stirring until small amount dropped into cold water forms a hard ball (256° on candy thermometer). Remove from heat. Add vanilla and pour into pan. When cool enough to handle, pull taffy until satiny and stiff. Color will lighten. Put a light coat of butter on hands to make handling easier. Put to 1/2 inch wide strips. Cut into pieces about 1-1/2 inches long and wrap in waxed paper.

Kathryn Hostetler

Casseroles
Meats & Soups

NOTES ON FAVORITE RECIPES

MEAT BALL STEW

1-1/2 lbs. ground beef	1 10 oz. can tomato soup
1 c. softened bread crumbs	1 10 oz. can beef broth
1 egg, beaten	6 potatoes - in 1 inch
1 tsp. salt	pieces
1/2 tsp. marjoram	8 small onions
1/4 tsp. thyme	2 tbsp. parsley - chopped
2 tbsp. oil	

Combine first 7 ingredients. Make into meat balls and brown in oil in large dutch oven. Remove them as they brown. Combine soups in pan. Add meat and vegetables and bring to boil. Cover and simmer for 30 minutes. Add parsley.

Marietta Cummins

YAMAZETTI

1 pkg. noodles	1 can evaporated milk
1/2 lb. yellow cheese	1 can tomato soup
1-1/2 lb. ground beef	1 green pepper chopped
	1 onion - chopped

Cook noodles for 10 minutes and drain. Brown meat and onion adding salt and pepper to taste. Place ingredients in a baking dish as follows: 1 layer noodles, 1 layer meat, 1 layer cheese, 1 layer green peppers. Repeat a second time. Add evaporated milk and soup. Bake for 1 hour at 375°. If too dry, add more milk.

Edna Mullet

DELICIOUS CASSEROLE

2 lbs. hamburger   2 cans cream of mushroom soup
1 pkg. noodles   2 cans tomato soup

Brown hamburger and drain. Cook noodles and drain. Mix all
ingredients in baking dish and bake at 375° for 1/2 hour.
Chopped onion may be added to meat if desired.

TATER TOT CASSEROLE

2 lbs. ground beef   3 boxes Tater Tots
1 onion - chopped   2 cans cream of mushroom soup
2 boxes frozen vegetables   Velveeta Cheese
2 cans cream of celery soup   1/4 c. milk

Brown beef and onions. Mix all ingredients together and place
in a baking dish. Put Velveeta cheese on top and bake at 350°
until very hot and bubbly. About 30 minutes.

Mrs. Susan Weaver

WIGGLERS CASSEROLE

3 lbs. hamburger
3 onions - chopped
3 c. cooked celery
2 cans cream of mushroom
  soup
2 cans peas
1 c. grated cheese

1-3/4 qt. tomato soup
1 lb. Velveeta cheese
2 sm. pkg. cooked
  spaghetti
9 slices bacon
3 c. diced cooked
  potatoes

Fry bacon in skillet, remove to plate and brown hamburger and onion in bacon fat. Put meat and onions in a six qt. casserole. Add potatoes, soup, carrots, and spaghetti. Arrange celery and bacon slices on top. Put grated cheese on top. Bake in moderate oven at 350° for 1 to 1-1/2 hours.

Mrs. Owen Schmucker

SHEPHERDS PIE

12 med. potatoes
3 lbs. ground beef
2 eggs
salt and pepper to taste

1 tsp. garlic salt
1/2 c. diced onions
Velveeta cheese
  milk

Cook and mash potatoes. Add milk, butter, salt and pepper as needed. Brown ground beef. Add all other ingredients to beef except for cheese and potatoes. Place meat mixture in the bottom of a deep baking dish and place mashed potatoes on top. Cover and bake at 375° for about 1 hour. Spread Velveeta cheese over top and put back in oven until it is hot and bubbly.

Mrs. Rebecca Miller

DELICIOUS ONE DISH DINNER

4 or 5 med. potatoes, sliced   1 lg. onion sliced
2 tbsp. butter   1 lb. hamburger
5 carrots, sliced   salt and pepper to taste

Place sliced potatoes in greased casserole. Arrange a layer of carrots and then a layer of onions on top of potatoes. Season with salt and pepper and slice butter across top. Make hamburger patties and place on top of vegetables. Add about 1/2 cup water. Cover tightly with aluminum foil and bake for one hour at 350°.

Ada J. Shrock

EASY TATER TOT CASSEROLE

2 cups corn flakes   1 box Tater Tots
2 eggs   1 can mushroom soup
2 lbs. ground beef   1 small onion
1-1/2 tsp. salt   1/8 tsp. pepper

Crush corn flakes; mix meat, corn flakes, beaten eggs, onion, salt and pepper. Put in baking dish. Top meat with Tater Tots and spread mushroom soup over top. Bake in oven at 350° for about one hour or until meat is done.

Liz Miller

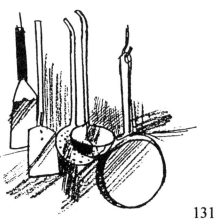

131

SAUCY WINTER CASSEROLE

1/4 lb. bacon, diced
1/2 c. chopped onion
4 tsp. Worcestershire sauce
1 c. Karo
3/4 tsp. salt
cooked macaroni
(6-8 servings)

1/4 tsp. paprika
3/4 c. water
1-1/2 c. tomato sauce
1 lb. wieners
1 tbsp. cornstarch
2 tbsp. water

Combine bacon and onion in skillet. Fry until bacon is crisp and onion is soft. Drain off extra fat. Stir in Worcestershire sauce, syrup, salt, paprika, water and tomato sauce. Bring to boil, reduce heat, cover and simmer 10 minutes. Add wieners and simmer until they are hot. Blend cornstarch with 2 tbsp. water, stir into the sauce and boil one minute. Serve on hot spaghetti or macaroni.

ZESTY MAIN DISH MIX-UP

1-1/2 lb. ground beef
1 c. chopped onion
1/2 c. chopped green pepper
1/2 tbsp. chili powder
1/3 clove garlic
2 c. beef gravy

2 c. kidney beans,
   drained
2 c. cooked macaroni
1/4 tsp. salt
1/8 tsp. pepper
1/2 c. shredded cheddar
   cheese

In skillet brown beef and cook onion and green pepper with chili powder and garlic until vegetables are tender. Add gravy, beans, macaroni, salt and pepper. Pour into 2 qt. baking dish (12x8x2). Bake at 450° for 15 minutes. Stir. Top with cheese; bake until cheese melts.

THREE LAYER DINNER

1 lb. hamburger	1 small cabbage
3 c. diced potatoes	1/2 tsp. salt
1/8 tsp. pepper	1 c. milk

Shred cabbage and put 1/2 of it in the bottom of a greased casserole. Next add 1/2 of potatoes and 1/2 of hamburger. Salt and pepper each layer. Add remaining ingredients in order having hamburger on top. Add milk and bake at 350° for 2 hours.

Mrs. Mahlon M. Byler

GREEN BEAN AND HAMBURGER CASSEROLE

1 lb. hamburger	1 can mushroom soup
2 chopped onions	mixed with
4 c. green beans	1 cup milk
1 pkg. Tater Tots	1 c. grated cheese

Brown hamburger and onions. Drain fat off and place hamburger in the bottom of a baking dish. Add green beans on top. Mix mushroom soup and milk and pour over the beans and hamburger. Place Tater Tots on top and bake at 350° until it starts to bubble, then turn down to 275° for an hour. Spread cheese across top.

Ella Byler

FAMILY DINNER CASSEROLE

1 lb. hamburger, broken up	1/2 c. uncooked rice
1-1/2 c. sliced potatoes	1-1/2 c. canned tomatoes
1/2 c. sliced onions	1 tsp. salt
1 c. sliced carrots	1/2 tsp. pepper
2 tbsp. sugar	

Partly cook hamburger and drain off fat. Place meat in 2-quart casserole and cover with layers of vegetables and rice. Add tomatoes with juice. Combine salt, pepper and sugar and sprinkle over top. Cover casserole and bake at 350° for 1-1/2 to 2 hours.

Ella Byler

STOVE TOP YUM-YUM CASSEROLE

2 lb. ground beef	1 onion, chopped
2 cans cream of mushroom soup	1 c. uncooked rice
	2 c. celery, diced
2 cans cream of chicken soup	3/4 c. water
	2 tbsp. soy sauce

Brown ground beef and chopped onion. Place in large saucepan. Add all other ingredients and mix well. Simmer until rice and celery are tender. Serve with chow mein noodles. Delicious!

Emma Shrock

MEAT LOAF - VEGETABLE CASSEROLE

Meat Loaf:

2 lb. ground beef	2 eggs, beaten
1 c. tomato juice	1/2 tsp. pepper
1-1/2 tsp. salt	1 onion, chopped
2 c. saltines, crushed	3 potatoes

Mix together and pat into bottom of a baking dish. Peel and slice 3 potatoes. Place on top of meat loaf. Mix the following:

2 cans vegetable soup   2 c. milk
2 cans cream of mushroom soup

Mix and pour over casserole, cutting through center so soup will go through evenly. Bake 2 hours at 350°. More milk may be added if it seems too thick. Very good!

Emma Shrock

THANK YOU CASSEROLE

5 potatoes	1 can vegetable soup
1 lb. hamburger	1 can cream of mushroom
1 onion - diced	soup

Slice potatoes into a buttered baking dish. Break up meat and mix into potatoes with soups and onion. Crumble a few potato chips over top and cover tightly. Bake at 375° for about 60 minutes.

HAMBURGER CASSEROLE

1-1/2 lb. hamburger
1 onion - chopped
2 tbsp. butter
1 pkg. noodles

1 pint sour cream
1 can peas
Salt and pepper to
taste

Brown meat and onions in butter. Cook noodles and drain. In a large pan or kettle, combine meat and noodles. Add sour cream, peas, salt and pepper. Heat and serve immediately.

Mrs. Allen Detweiler

DELICIOUS HAMBURGER IN CASSEROLE

1 lb. ground beef
1 lg. onion - chopped
10-1/2 oz. can tomato soup
1/2 c. warm milk
1 tsp. salt
*Lard may be substituted with butter

2 tbsp. lard
1/2 qt. green beans
5 medium potatoes -
cooked
1 egg - beaten

Brown beef and onions in lard. Add green beans and tomato soup. Mix thoroughly and pour into greased baking dish. Mash potatoes and add milk, egg, salt and pepper. Pour on top of meat mixture. Bake in 350° oven for 30 minutes.

Barbara Weaver

POT LUCK CHEESE AND POTATO CASSEROLE

2 lbs. jacket boiled potatoes, peeled and chopped
4 tbsp. melted butter
1 tsp. salt
1/4 tsp. pepper
1 pt. sour cream
1 can cream of chicken soup undiluted
2 c. grated, sharp cheddar cheese
2 c. crushed corn flakes, mixed with 1/4 c. melted butter
1/2 c. chopped onion

Combine potatoes and butter in a large mixing bowl. Add salt, pepper, onion, soup, sour cream, cheese. Blend thoroughly. Pour into greased casserole 9x13. Cover with crushed corn flakes mixed with melted butter. Bake 350° for 45 minutes.

HAMBURGER VEGETABLE CASSEROLE

3 lbs. hamburger
6 lg. potatoes - sliced thick
6 carrots - sliced
1 onion - chopped
1 can cream of mushroom soup
1 can cream of chicken soup
1 pt. sour cream

Place vegetables in layers in buttered baking dish. Crumble raw hamburger over top. Pour soups and sour cream over all. Bake at 375° until potatoes are done.

Mrs. Emma Weaver

QUICK DINNER

Make a medium sized hamburger and put on top of one thinly sliced potato. Add a few slices of carrot and a slice of onion. Add salt, pepper and catsup to taste Place all in foil and wrap tight. Cook on grill or in 375° oven until done.

Mrs. Betty Shrock

CHILI

5 lbs. ground beef
1 c. onion - chopped
1 c. celery - chopped
1 tsp. chili powder
3 tbsp. salt and pepper

3 gal. water
1 gal. tomato puree
1 c. corn starch
2 gal. kidney beans
1-1/2 tbsp. chili powder

Brown meat, onions, celery and 1 tsp. chili powder in very large pot. Add water, tomato puree, 1-1/2 tsp. chili powder and salt. Let mixture come to a boil. Thicken with corn starch and then add kidney beans. Makes a very large batch.

Mrs. Elmer L. Yoder

BARBECUED BEEF SANDWICHES

1/2 c. chopped onion
4 tbsp. sugar
1/2 tsp. pepper
1/2 c. catsup
1/4 c. water

3 tbsp. vinegar
1 tsp. Worcestershire
   sauce
2 lbs. cooked chopped
   chunk beef

Mix all ingredients except beef and cook over low heat for 5 minutes. Add cooked beef. Serve hot on buns.

Edna D. Yoder

138

SPANISH RICE

1 lb. hamburger	1 green pepper
4 c. cooked rice	2 tbsp. shortening
2 sm. onions	1 tsp. salt
1 c. tomatoes	1 tsp. chili powder

Chop onions and pepper and cook in fat until brown. Add hamburger, salt, pepper and chili powder. When meat is slightly brown, place layers of cooked rice and meat mixture in a casserole. Pour tomatoes over contents of dish and bake at 375° for about 50 minutes.

Edna D. Yoder

OVEN BARBECUED HAMBURGERS

1-1/2 lb. ground beef	3 tbsp. onion - chopped
3/4 c. rolled oats	1-1/2 tsp. salt
1 c. milk	1/4 tsp. pepper

Mix all ingredients and make medium sized patties. Brown in small amount of cooking oil and set aside. Make the following sauce.

BARBECUE SAUCE

1 tbsp. Worcestershire sauce	1/2 c. water
2 tbsp. sugar	1 c. catsup
3 tbsp. vinegar	6 tbsp. onion - chopped

Mix all ingredients. Place browned patties in baking pan and pour sauce over them. Bake for 1 hour at 350°. Serve on buns. Delicious!

Emma Shrock

MOCK STEAK WITH GRAVY

3 lbs. ground beef
1 c. soda crackers - crushed
1 c. water
1 tsp. steak sauce
1 c. water

2 tsp. salt
2 cans cream of mushroom
  soup
2 tbsp. flour

Mix ground beef, crackers, salt and water. Form into roll and refrigerate overnight. Next day, slice meat and brown in a skillet. Place slices in covered baking dish. Mix cream of mushroom soup, flour, steak sauce, and second cup of water and pour over meat. Bake at 350° for 1 to 1-1/2 hours. Very good!

Emma Shrock

WESTERN BEANS WITH HAMBURGER

1 lb. hamburger
1 pkg. onion soup mix
1/2 c. water
1 c. catsup

2 tsp. mustard
2 tsp. vinegar
2 cans pork'n beans
  (1 lb. 2 oz.)

Brown hamburger, mix the rest of the ingredients, then simmer slowly for a couple of hours. Simmer over very low heat until done.

Mrs. Harvey W. Byler

140

BAR-B-Q BEEF

2 tbsp. butter
1 onion - chopped
1 qt. cooked beef - chunked
1 tbsp. vinegar
2 tbsp. brown sugar
1 tsp. salt

1/2 tsp. pepper
2 tsp. paprika
1 tsp. chili powder
1/2 c. catsup or Open
  Pit barbecue sauce
1/2 c. water

Mix all ingredients together in a pan and cook slowly for 20 minutes.

Mrs. Sam Detweiler

VEAL POT PIE

2 tbsp. cooking oil
3 lbs. boneless veal - cut
  into 3 in. cubes

2 tsp. salt
1/2 tsp. pepper
3-1/2 c. boiling water

Brown veal in hot oil in a dutch oven. This takes 15-20 minutes. Add salt and pepper. Add water, reduce heat and simmer 45 minutes or until meat is tender. While meat is cooking, make the following:

DUMPLING SQUARES

1-1/2 c. flour	3/4 c. onion - coarsely
1/2 tsp. salt	chopped
1 tsp. baking powder	3 c. diced potatoes
1-1/2 tsp. butter	3 tbsp. chopped parsley
1 egg, beaten	1 tsp. paprika

Sift flour, salt and baking powder into bowl. Cut in butter until particles are size of peas (use pastry blender or two knives). Using a fork, quickly stir in egg and 3 to 4 tbsp. cold water. Dough will be stiff. Roll dough out to 1/2 in. thick to form a rectangle approximately 12x6 inches. Using a sharp knife, cut dough into 1-1/2 in. squares. Let stand uncovered for several minutes. Meanwhile, add onion, potatoes, parsley and paprika to veal, in dutch oven. Simmer covered for 10 minutes.

Remove cover; drop half of dumpling squares, one by one, into simmering liquid. As they drop to the bottom of the dutch oven, add the rest of the squares, stirring carefully.

Simmer, covered, 25 minutes, or until dumplings are light and cooked through. Sprinkle top with more chopped parsley.

Makes 6 to 8 servings.

Eileen Miller

AMISH WISDOM

Some people eat for nutrition,
some people eat for the taste.
Some eat just for the fun of it,
and most of it goes to waist.

******

MEAT BALL STEW

1-1/2 lbs. ground beef
1 c. softened bread crumbs
1 egg - beaten
1 tsp. salt
1/2 tsp. marjoram
1/4 tsp. thyme
2 tbsp. cooking oil
8 sm. white onions

1 lg. can tomato soup
(10-1/2 oz.)
1 lg. can condensed beef
broth (10-1/2 oz.)
6 med potatoes
6 carrots - scraped and
sliced into 1 in. pcs.
2 tbsp. chopped parsley

Combine first seven ingredients. Shape into 24 meatballs.
Brown meat in cooking oil in a 4 qt. dutch oven. Remove as
they brown. Combine soup and broth in dutch oven. Add meat
and vegetables. Bring to a boil. Cover and simmer for 30 min.
or until vegetables are tender. Add parsley. Serves 6 to 8.

Mrs. Marietta Cummins

MEAT AND POTATO SKILLET

1 can luncheon meat such
as Spam
1 onion - sliced thinly
2 tbsp. lard
1 can cream of mushroom
soup

1/2 c. milk
2 c. potatoes, cubed
and cooked
2 tbsp. parsley -
chopped
dash of pepper

Cut luncheon meat into bite-sized pieces and brown with sliced
onions in lard. Blend in mushroom soup and milk. Add
potatoes, parsley and pepper. Cook over low heat about 10
minutes. Very good!

Susan Gingerich

DELICIOUS HAM AND CAULIFLOWER

1 can cream of celery soup   1 c. diced ham (cooked)
1/2 c. milk   buttered bread crumbs

Mix soup and milk together. Pour over cooked cauliflower. Add diced ham and mix lightly. Pour into casserole. Sprinkle bread crumbs over top. Bake in oven at 375° for 1/2 hour or until bread crumbs are browned.

HAM LOAF

3/4 lb. ham - smoked and   1/2 c. milk
  ground   1/2 c. bread crumbs
1/4 lb. fresh pork - ground   1/8 tsp. pepper
1 egg - beaten

Mix all ingredients thoroughly. Shape into two loaves in shallow baking pan. Bake 1 hour or until done in 350° oven. Makes 4 servings.

GERMAN SNITZ AND KNEPP

1/2 ham   4 c. flour
1 handful dried apples   2 eggs, beaten
2 slices bacon   milk
2 tsp. salt

Cut ham into small chunks. Brown in dutch oven, along with bacon pieces. Add a small amount of water and cook until ham is very tender. Add apples the last hour of cooking.
When ham and apples are nearly done, bring a 6 qt. sauce pan of water to a boil. Add 2 teaspoons of salt. Mix the flour, 2 tsp. salt, eggs and enough milk to make a stiff batter. Drop into boiling water by teaspoonfuls, and cook for 20 minutes.
When dumplings are done, add them to the ham and apples and simmer. Serve piping hot.

Mrs. William C. Hochstetler

SPARERIBS AND SAUERKRAUT

4 lbs. or 2 sides spareribs
salt and pepper
1 qt. sauerkraut
1 apple, chopped

2 tbsp. brown sugar
1 tbsp. caraway seeds
1 onion, sliced
2 c. water

Cut ribs and brown in skillet and season. Pour off fat. Place kraut mixed with apples, sugar, caraway and onion in a kettle. Place ribs on top. Pour water around meat and kraut. Cover tightly and simmer 1-1/4 to 1-1/2 hours or until ribs are very tender.

MINCE MEAT

1 qt. ground meat
2 qt. sliced apples
2 qt. cider (or grape juice)
1 qt. sour cherries
5 c. sugar
salt to taste

1/2 tsp. cinnamon
1/4 tsp. ground cloves
1/4 tsp. all spice
juice and rind of 2
    oranges
2 c. raisins

Mix all ingredients and cook 15 minutes. Stir frequently to prevent scorching. Add more cider if necessary. Pour into hot sterilized jars and seal at once. Process 30 minutes in hot bath.

SALMON SOUFFLE

Mince 1 can of salmon
2 egg yolks
1-1/4 c. milk

1 c. bread crumbs
1/2 tsp. vinegar

Mix all together, add beaten egg whites. Put in casserole. Bake 30 minutes in 400° oven.

SALMON PATTIES

2 c. cracker crumbs
1 c. salmon
1 tsp. salt (scant)

2 eggs beaten
1-1/2 c. milk
pepper to taste

Roll crackers until fine. Mix with other ingredients. Drop by tablespoons and fry in butter.

HOT DOG ON A STICK

1-1/2 c. flour
1/2 tsp. salt
1-1/2 tsp. baking powder
2 tbsp. sugar

1/2 c. cornmeal
3/4 c. milk
1 egg
hot dogs

Mix all ingredients together. Insert a wooden stick in hot dog. Dip hot dog into batter and deep fry in oil at 375° until golden brown.

Alma Miller

PIGS IN BLANKETS

12 wieners
2 slices American cheese
  cut into 12 strips
1/4 c. pickle relish
3 c. pancake mix

mustard
1 tsp. barbecue seasoning
1/2 c. shortening
1 c. milk

Slice wieners lengthwise. Fill each with a strip of cheese and 1 tsp. relish. Put pancake mix and seasoning in a bowl and cut in the shortening until coarse crumbs are formed. Add milk until mixture is dampened and turn dough out on board. Knead gently. Divide dough into 2 parts. Roll out to about 1/4 inch thick. Cut each into 6 squares. Spread with mustard and wrap wieners. Seal edges well and bake in 350° oven, 15 to 20 minutes or until nicely browned.

Liz Miller

SCALLOPED WIENERS

1 lb. wieners
5 c. crackers (coarsely
  crushed)
2 eggs

4-1/2 c. milk
pepper to taste
4 lg. tbsp. butter
2 tsp. salt

Add a small amount of water to the wieners and cook for 10
minutes. Slice the wieners. Make alternate layers of crackers
and wieners in a casserole. Beat egg and add seasoning and
milk. Pour over crackers and wieners. Dot the top with butter.
Bake at 450° for 3 minutes or until done. This will fill a very
large casserole or 2 smaller ones.

DELICIOUS FRIED CHICKEN

1 whole chicken
1 egg
2/3 c. water
1/4 c. cooking oil
3/4 c. flour

2 tsp. salt
1 tsp. paprika
dash of red pepper and
  black

Beat egg, water and cooking oil together. Add salt, paprika,
peppers and flour and mix until smooth. Dip cut up chicken into
batter and roll in flour. Fry in enough hot oil to cover. Turn
chicken often while frying. Fry for 30-45 minutes until golden
brown and crisp.

Mrs. Melvin C. Miller

AMISH WISDOM

*An apology is often a good way
to have the last word.*

*****

CHICKEN AND DUMPLINGS

1 chicken - preferably a
  4 lb. hen
1 tsp. salt
water to cover
4 medium-sized potatoes,
  sliced
2 tbsp. parsley

For dumpling dough:
2 c. flour
1/2 tsp. salt
2 eggs
2-3 tablespoons water

Cut chicken into serving pieces and cook until tender. Season
with salt. When chicken is almost soft, add the sliced potatoes.

To make dumplings, make a well in the flour and add the eggs
and salt. Work together into a stiff dough; if too dry add water
or milk. Roll out the dough as thin as possible (1/8 in.) and cut
in 1 inch squares with a knife or pastry wheel. Drop into the
boiling broth, which should be sufficient to cover the chicken
well. Add the chopped parsley. Some flour can be added to
broth to make like gravy. Serves 6-8.

Anna Marie Weaver

148

BARBECUED CHICKEN

Barbecue Sauce:

1 tsp. salt	1 c. catsup
1/4 tsp. pepper	1 med. onion - minced
1 tbsp. paprika	1/2 c. water
1 tbsp sugar	1/3 c. lemon juice or
1/2 tsp. garlic salt	vinegar
1 tbsp. Worcestershire sauce	1/4 c. butter

In a saucepan, blend salt, pepper, paprika, sugar and garlic salt. Add remaining ingredients. Heat to boiling and then remove from heat. Makes 2-1/2 cups.

Coating:
For each pound of chicken, blend:

1/4 c. flour	pinch of pepper
1 tsp. salt	1 tsp. paprika

Coat cut up chicken with seasoned flour. Brown in skillet containing at least 1/2 inch of fat. Then dip browned chicken in barbecue sauce and place on a baking sheet. Bake in 350° oven until tender.

Mrs. Emma Weaver

HUMOROUS AMISH SAYINGS

If a rooster crows,
'fore goin' to bed,
he's shore to wake up
with a wet head. (rain)

149

CHICKEN-N-STUFF

Dressing:

6 c. bread crumbs, browned   1 tsp. onion, chopped
1/4 c. celery - chopped   2 eggs
1 tsp. parsley flakes   1/4 c. butter
salt and pepper to taste

Mix all ingredients and add enough hot water to moisten. Place in a greased casserole.

Cream Topping:

1/4 c. butter   1 can cream of celery
1 c. chicken broth   soup
1 can cream of chicken   2 c. cooked chicken
  soup   salt and pepper

Melt butter and thicken with flour. Add milk, salt and pepper. Cook until thick gravy. Add chicken broth and soups. Pour over dressing. Bake at 350° for 45 minutes.

Lydia Troyer

CHICKEN AND CHEESE CASSEROLE

3 c. cubed chicken   1 tbsp. chicken boullion
1 c. macaroni - uncooked   cubes
1/2 c. onion - chopped   2-1/2 c. milk
1/4 c. butter   2 tbsp. pimentos -
1/4 c. flour   chopped
1-1/2 c. shredded cheese   1 c. buttered bread
                                crumbs

Cook onions in butter until tender. Stir in flour and boullion, stir in milk and cook until sauce thickens. Then add cheese and cook until melted. Remove from stove and combine chicken, macaroni and pimentos; add sauce. Put in 2 qt. baking dish. Cover with crumbs and bake at 350° for 1 hour.

Mrs. Chris Troyer

OLD FASHIONED POT PIE

1 qt. broth, chicken or beef   Dough;
1 c. celery, minced   1/2 c. milk
2 potatoes, peeled and   1/4 tsp. salt
   diced   1/4 tsp. baking powder
     1 1/2 c. flour

Add potatoes and celery to broth. Season with salt and pepper to taste. Mix dough ingredients. Add enough flour to make the dough stiff. Roll thin and cut into small squares. When broth starts to boil, add dough squares separately and keep boiling while adding. When all the squares have been added, cook for 10-15 minutes. Stir occasionally. Cook on low heat for 10-15 minutes more.

Mrs. Chris M. Troyer

SMOTHERED HAM

1 c. bread crumbs   dash of pepper
1 c. milk   several whole cloves
1 minced onion   1/4 c. brown sugar
1/2 tsp. salt   1 c. water
2 inch ham slice

Place all ingredients on top of a 2 inch raw ham slice and bake in oven for three hours at 400°.

Mrs. Ervin E. Yoder

BARBECUED CHIP CHOP HAM

3/4 c. catsup
1/2 c. water
1 tbsp. Worcestershire sauce
1 lb. chipped ham

1 tsp. vinegar
1 tbsp. sugar
1-1/2 tsp. mustard

Bring sauce to boil. Drop chipped ham into sauce, one slice at a time. Reduce heat and cook until meat is hot. Serve on toasted buns.

Mrs. Chris M. Troyer

SAUSAGE LOAF

1-1/2 lb. pork sausage
1-1/2 c. bread or cracker
 crumbs
2 tbsp. grated onion
2 tbsp. catsup

2 tbsp. horseradish
2 tsp. prepared mustard
1 egg slightly beaten
1/2 c. milk

Mix sausage and cracker crumbs, add onion, catsup, horseradish, mustard and egg. Moisten with milk. Shape into loaf and bake at 350° for 1 hour.

HUMOROUS AMISH SAYINGS

A whistlin' woman,
and crowin' hen,
are shore to cum,
to some bad end.

BAKED TUNA CHEESE CASSEROLE

1 c. macaroni, cooked
1 tbsp. butter
1/4 c. onion, chopped
1/8 tsp. pepper
1 tsp. dry mustard
2-1/2 tbsp. flour

small pkg. frozen peas
 and carrots
2 c. milk
2 6-1/2 oz. cans tuna
 fish
Velveeta cheese

Brown onions in butter until golden. Add flour, salt, pepper and mustard. Slowly add milk until mixture is smooth and has thickened. Add tuna, cooked macaroni and peas and carrots. Pour all into a casserole and cover top with thin slices of Velveeta cheese. Bake at 375° for about 40 minutes. Makes 6 servings.

Mrs. Ervin E. C. Miller

TUNA SURPRISE

1 6-1/2 oz. can tuna
1 tbsp. sugar
salt and pepper to taste

3 tbsp. salad dressing
1/2 tsp. onion, minced

Mix all ingredients. Put between sandwich buns. Wrap separately in aluminum foil and bake in 375° oven for 15 minutes.

Mrs. Jonas Stutzman

AMISH OMELET

3 eggs, beaten	1/2 tsp. salt
1/2 c. flour	dash of pepper
1 pint of milk	

Beat all ingredients until smooth. Pour into buttered frying pan and cook over moderate heat until set. Turn once.

This omelet can also be baked in a buttered casserole, at 350°, until brown. No need to turn it.

Mrs. W. J. Hochstetler

QUICK SALMON SOUP

Brown 2 or 3 tbsp. butter in a saucepan. Add about 3 qts. milk, salt and pepper to taste. When it begins to boil, add 1 can salmon, chopped. Heat and serve with crackers or toasted bread cubes.

VEGETABLE BEEF SOUP

1-1/2 lbs. beef, in chunks	1 lg. onion,, chopped
1 lg. can tomatoes	6 or 8 carrots, sliced
3 stalks celery, chopped	5 potatoes, cut up
1/2 cabbage, cut up	1/2 tsp. celery seed
1/2 c. rice	1 tsp. sugar
1 soup bone	salt and pepper to taste

Cover beef and bone with water and simmer about 1-1/2 hours or until done. Remove bone and add vegetables in order given. Cook until vegetables and rice are done, about 45 minutes.

Mrs. Herman Yoder

AMISH BEAN SOUP

Brown 2 or 3 tbsp. butter in saucepan. Add 1 cup cooked beans and 1/4 cup water. Bring to a boil, then add about 3 qts. milk, salt and pepper to taste. Add a dash of allspice. Boil, then remove from stove. Add about 2 quarts stale, thinly sliced bread, or enough to thicken. Cover and let stand about 1/2 hour before serving. Serve with pickled red beets or pickles.

HAM SOUP

4 c. ham (cubed)	4 medium potatoes
3/4 c. onion, minced	3 qts. milk
1 c. noodles, dry	

Combine ham and onions. Saute' until ham is tender. Cut potatoes into small cubes and cook in small amount of water until tender. Drain. Cook noodles in salt water until soft, and drain. Add to ham along with potatoes and the milk. Bring to a boil and add salt and pepper. Serve with crackers or corn bread.

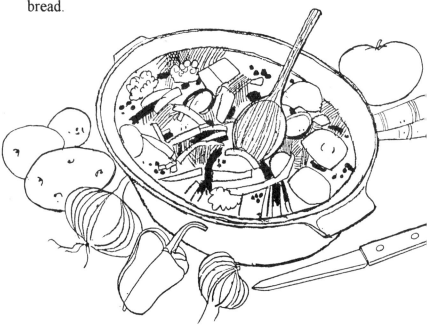

BROWN-FLOUR POTATO SOUP

3 c. diced pared potatoes
  (1 lb.)
1/2 c. chopped onion
1/4 c. unsifted all-purpose
  flour

2 tsp. salt
1/8 tsp. pepper
2 hard cooked eggs,
1 tbsp. chopped parsley
1 tbsp. butter or margarine

In a large saucepan, bring 1 inch slightly salted water to boiling.
Add potatoes and onion; cook, covered, until tender - about ten
minutes. Add milk; bring to boiling. Meanwhile, in small, heavy
skillet, slowly heat flour, stirring, until flour is light golden.
Blend i butter. Stir, over low heat, until mixture is well
browned. Stir browned flour into milk; bring to boiling. Reduce
heat and simmer until slightly thickened. Add salt, pepper and
chopped egg. Sprinkle with parsley. Serve hot. Makes 6
servings.

Mrs. Eileen Miller

156

CHICKEN AND CORN SOUP

4 lbs. roasting chicken
  cut up
2 tsp. salt
dash of pepper
1/4 tsp. saffron
1 stalk celery, with leaves
1 whole onion, peeled

1 c. medium noodles
2 pkgs. (10 oz. size)
  frozen whole-kernel
  corn
2 tsp. chopped parsley
2 hard-cooked eggs,
  coarsely chopped

Rinse chicken well in cold water. Place in 4 qt. kettle along with 2 qts. water, the salt, pepper, saffron, celery and onion. Bring to boiling, reduce heat and simmer, covered, 1 hour or until chicken is tender. Skim off fat. Lift out chicken, let cool slightly. Remove celery and onion and discard. Remove chicken from bones, cut into bite-size pieces. Return chicken to broth; bring to boiling. Add noodles and corn; boil, uncovered, 20 minutes or until noodles are tender. If necessary, add a little more salt and pepper. Just before serving, add parsley and chopped egg. Makes 6 to 8 servings.

Mrs. Eileen Miller

WINTER VEGETABLE SOUP

1 qt. beef broth
2 c. green beans
2 c. carrots
2 c. cabbage
2 c. peas
1 c. navy beans, cooked

2 c. corn
2 c. celery
2 c. lima beans
2 c. tomatoes
2 tbsp. salt
1 c. water

Chop celery, carrots, cabbage and green beans. Combine with other ingredients in a large soup pot. Cook for 2-1/2 to 3 hours on medium heat so that it stays at a low boil. Delicious served with hot corn bread or biscuits.

GERMAN CABBAGE SOUP

2 cans (10-1/2 oz. ea.)
  condensed beef broth
2-1/2 c. water
2 tsp. lemon juice
2 c. diced apples
1 tbsp. caraway seed
1/4 tsp. garlic powder or
  1 fresh clove crushed garlic

1 can (8 oz.) tomato
  sauce
3 c. shredded cabbage
1/3 c. sliced onions
1 tsp. sugar
1/8 tsp. black pepper

In large saucepan combine all ingredients except apples, cabbage, onions and spices. Bring to a boil. Add spices, apples, and vegetables. Cover and simmer 30 minutes or until cabbage is tender. Serves 6-8.

Mrs. Emma Byler

CABBAGE CHOWDER

4 c. coarsely shredded
  cabbage
2 c. sliced carrots
3 c. diced potatoes
3 c. water

1 tbsp. salt
1/2 tsp. sugar
1/4 tsp. pepper
4 c. scalded milk
2 tsp. butter

Cook vegetables and seasonings in water until tender. Add the scalded milk and butter. Serve with crackers.

RIVVEL SOUP

1 c. flour
1/2 tsp. salt

1 egg
1 qt. milk

Mix salt with the flour, then toss egg lightly through flour with fork until small crumbs form. Stir into 1 quart of scalding whole milk. Bring to a boil and serve at once.

Edna Mullet

TOMATO SOUP

1/2 bushel tomatoes	14 tsp. flour
2 qts. water	16 tbsp. sugar
7 med. onions, chopped	4 tbsp. paprika
11 sprigs parsley	8 tbsp. salt
14 stalks celery, diced	1 pint water
14 tbsp. melted butter	

Bring sliced, unpeeled tomatoes and 2 quarts water to boil. Add chopped onions, parsley, diced celery. Cook until vegetables are well done. Run through sieve. Put back in pan to cook. Add butter, flour, sugar, paprika and salt. Add 1 pint of water and cook until thick. Strain if necessary. Put in sterilized one-quart jars and seal. Dilute with 1/2 to 1 pint milk or water when you open jars to heat.

Mrs. Rebecca Miller

CABBAGE STEW

1 head cabbage	2 lb. cubed beef
5 carrots	salt and pepper to taste
1/2 c. celery	1 onion

Cut cabbage into chunks; slice carrots thick; add diced celery and sliced onion. Add cubed beef, salt and pepper. Add about 1 pint water. Bring to a boil and simmer about 1-1/2 hours or until meat is tender. Add water if necessary.

PARSLEY DUMPLINGS

1-1/2 c. sifted all purpose
  flour
2 tsp. baking powder
1/2 tsp. salt
1-1/2 tbsp. chopped parsley

1 tbsp. butter or
  margarine, melted
1 egg, beaten
1/3 to 1/2 c. milk

Into medium bowl sift flour, baking powder, salt. Stir in parsley.
With fork, stir in butter and egg. Add 1/3 c. milk, stirring. If
mixture seems dry, add a little more milk. Dumpling mixture
should be stiff, but moist.) Cook dumplings as directed above.
Makes enough for 6 servings.

Mrs. Eileen Miller

BROWN HAM GRAVY

1/4 c. unsifted all-purpose
  flour
1/4 c. dark brown sugar,
  firmly packed

1-1/2 c. cooking liquid
  from ham

In medium saucepan, over low heat, brown flour, stirring
constantly until deep golden. Remove from heat. Stir in sugar.
Gradually add ham liquid, stirring to make smooth mixture.
Bring to boiling, stirring constantly. Makes about one cup.

Mrs. Eileen Miller

WASHDAY DINNER

1 tbsp. butter	1 lg. can tomato juice
3 onions, sliced	2 tbsp. flour
6 potatoes, sliced	boiling water
8 sausage links	salt to taste
2 tbsp. flour	

Use a large flat pan. Cover bottom with butter. Line the bottom of the pan with thick layer of onion slices; then add generous layer of sliced potatoes. Sift 2 tbsp. flour over this. Pour can of tomato juice over whole. Slice sausages thinly to cover the top. Add enough boiling water to cover. Add salt to taste. Bake slowly for 3 hours. If sausages begin to get too brown, turn them over.

Edna Mullet

HEARTY HAMBURGER SOUP

1 tbsp. butter	1 c. diced potatoes
1 c. chopped onion	1-1/2 tsp. salt
1 c. sliced carrot	1 tsp. seasoned salt
1/2 c. chopped green pepper	1/2 tsp. pepper
1 lb. ground beef	1/3 c. flour
2 c. tomato juice	4 c. milk

Melt butter in saucepan; brown meat; add onion and cook until transparent. Stir in remaining ingredients except flour and milk. Cover and cook over low heat until vegetables are tender. Combine flour with 1 c. of milk. Stir into soup mixture. Boil. Add remaining milk and heat, stirring frequently. Do not boil after remaining milk.

This recipe can be adapted to your family's taste. Celery can be substituted for the green pepper if you wish.

EASY NOODLE CASSEROLE

2 lb. hamburger
2 chopped onions
1/2 pkg. noodles, cooked
1 pint corn

2 cans mushroom soup
1 c. sour cream
2 pkgs. frozen peas
1 c. bread crumbs
4 tbsp. melted butter

Brown meat and onions. Mix cooked noodles, peas and corn together with mushroom soup and sour cream. Put all in casserole. Mix bread crumbs with butter and spread on top. Bake in 350° oven for 45 minutes.

Mrs. Joe Weaver

EGG NOODLE CASSEROLE

1 lb. hamburger
1 12 oz. pkg. egg noodles
1 10-1/2 oz. can mushroom
  soup
1 10-1/2 oz. can celery soup

1/2 tsp. salt
1/2 tsp. pepper
1/2 small onion - chopped
1/2 green pepper - chopped
1/2 tsp. garlic salt

Brown meat, onion and green peppers. Cook noodles and drain. Combine noodles, meat, celery soup, mushroom soup, salt, pepper and garlic salt. Top with cracker crumbs and bake at 350° for 35-40 minutes or until hot and brown on top.

Lucie Byler

AMISH CASSEROLE

1 lg. pkg. noodles
2 c. peas
1 can cr. of mushroom soup
1/2 loaf of bread - toasted
  and made into crumbs

1 c. sour cream
3 lb. hamburger
1 can cream of chicken
  soup
1 onion chopped

Cook noodles and drain. Brown hamburger and onion in butter.
Place meat, peas and noodles in a baking dish. Pour soups and
sour cream over them and put buttered bread crumbs on top.
Bake for 1 hour at 375°.

Susan Gingerich

STUFFED CABBAGE ROLLS

1 lb. ground beef
8 cabbage leaves
1-1/2 c. soft bread crumbs
1/2 c. finely chopped onion
1-1/2 tsp. salt

1/2 tsp. garlic salt
1/4 tsp. pepper
1 can tomato soup
2 eggs

Wilt cabbage leaves by placing them in boiling water for 3
minutes and then drain. Mix all other ingredients except soup.
Shape meat mixture into oblong rolls and wrap in cabbage
leaves. Fasten with toothpicks. Put tomato soup in a skillet and
add rolls. Bring to a boil, then reduce heat and simmer for 45 -
60 minutes or until meat mixture is well done. You may need to
add a little water during cooking period. Serve immediately.

Mrs. Dan T. Yoder

STUFFED PEPPERS

1/2 lb. hamburger
1 onion, chopped
1 egg
1/2 c. cooked rice

1 can tomato sauce
salt and pepper to taste
4 green peppers

Mix all ingredients together except tomato sauce and put in peppers which have been hollowed out and washed. Pour sauce over top and bake in moderate oven until done. About one hour.

Mrs. Elmer Dan Yoder

POTATO CABBAGE CASSEROLE

4-5 potatoes, sliced
1 med. onion, sliced
8 c. chopped cabbage
2 tbsp. butter
1/2 c. boiling water

2 tsp. salt
1/4 tsp. pepper
1 pkg. wieners - cut in
1 inch pieces

Placed potato slices in large skillet. Place layer of onions on top. Place layer of cabbage on onions. Mix butter with 1/2 c. boiling water and pour over vegetables. Cook until tender. Put parmesan cheese on top, cover, and bake for 25-30 minutes in 375° oven. Sprinkle with paprika.

Marietta Cummins

SOUR CREAM CABBAGE

4 c. finely grated cabbage 2 tbsp. sour cream
1 tsp. flour salt and pepper

Simmer cabbage in tightly-covered saucepan with small amount of water until soft. Sprinkle flour over the cabbage. Add 2 tbsp. of sour cream and salt and pepper to taste. Mix well. Heat through for a couple of minutes and serve.

CORN MEAL MUSH

3/4 c. cornmeal 2 tbsp. margarine
3/4 c. cold water 3/4 tsp. salt
2-1/2 c. boiling water

Mix cornmeal and cold water in saucepan. Stir in boiling water and salt. Cook, stirring constantly until mixture boils. Reduce heat. Cover and simmer 10 minutes. Spread in deep greased baking dish or loaf pan. Cover and refrigerate until firm - at least 12 hours. Cut in slices, fry in margarine over low heat until brown. Serve with maple syrup.

Katherine M. Byler

SWEET AND SOUR BAKED BEANS

1 onion 30 oz. butter beans
1-1/2 c. brown sugar 16 oz. green lima beans
1 tsp. dry mustard 16 oz. baked beans
1/2 tsp. garlic 16 oz. red kidney beans
1 tsp. salt 8 slices bacon, fried
1/2 c. vinegar   and crumbled

Boil onion, brown sugar, dry mustard, garlic salt, salt and vinegar together about 15 minutes. Drain butter beans, and lima beans; do not drain baked beans or kidney beans. Pour boiled ingredients over all beans and mix in bacon. Bake at 350° for one hour.

SPICED BEETS

1 gal. small beets
3 c. vinegar
1 qt. water
2 c. sugar

1-1/2 sticks cinnamon
1 tbsp. all spice
1-1/2 tsp. salt

Cook beets. Bring vinegar mixture to boil. Put beets in hot sterilized jars; then add boiling mixture and seal.

Mrs. Rebecca Miller

CRUSTY BAKED POTATOES

6 medium potatoes
4 tbsp. melted butter

1/2 c. cracker crumbs
1 tsp. salt

Peel, wash and wipe potatoes. Cut in halves. Roll in melted butter and in cracker crumbs on which salt has been added. Place in greased pan and bake 1 hour at 350°.

Mrs. Dan J. M. Miller

FAST VEGETABLE SCALLOPED DISH

1 can (or 16 oz. jar) lima
  beans
1 can (or 12 oz. jar) whole
  kernel corn, drained
1/2 tsp. celery salt

1 can (or 16 z. jar)
  tomatoes
5 tbsp. butter
1/2 tsp. onion salt

In a one and one-half quart casserole combine all ingredients except butter. Dot surface with butter. Bake in moderate oven at 350° for 1/2 hour or more.

Ella Byler

CINNAMON YAMS

2 tbsp. lt. brown sugar
1/2 tsp. cinnamon
1/4 tsp. salt

2 18 oz. canned yams,
   drained
2 tbsp. butter, melted

Combine brown sugar with salt and cinnamon. Slice yams lengthwise 1/4 inch thick. Place a layer of yams in a casserole (shallow). Sprinkle some of the brown sugar mixture over the tops and spoon some melted butter on. Repeat layering until all yams and sugar are used. Bake in 350° oven for about 25 minutes.

FRENCH FRIED ONION RINGS

3 large onions
1/2 c. milk
1 egg

3/4 c. flour
1/2 tsp. salt

Mix batter; dip in onion rings and fry in oil 375° until brown.

Susan Gingerich

PATCHES

Grind or grate six medium-sized raw, peeled potatoes and drain in a colander. Stir in 2 tbsp. flour and milk to make a thin batter. Add salt and pepper to taste. Parsley and onion may be added. Fry in well-oiled skillet.

BASQUE POTATOES

1/2 c. finely chopped onion
1/2 c. chopped celery
1/2 c. shredded carrot
1 clove garlic, minced
salt and pepper to taste

parsley, chopped
2 c. chicken broth
4 c. potatoes, pared and
  cubed

Saute onion, celery, carrot and garlic in melted butter in a 10 inch skillet until tender. Add chicken broth, potatoes, salt and pepper to sauteed vegetables. Cover; simmer for 10 minutes. Remove cover. Simmer, stirring occasionally, 20 minutes or until broth is thickened. Sprinkle with parsley. Makes 4 to 6 servings.

ZUCCHINI SQUASH CASSEROLE

3 c. diced zucchini
1/2 c. celery - diced
1 onion - diced

1-1/2 c. tomato juice
1/2 c. toasted bread crumbs
cheese slices

Make layers of squash, onion, celery and sliced cheese, ending with cheese. Top with bread crumbs. Pour the tomato juice over the top and bake in 350° oven for 1 hour or until done.

Mrs. Mahlon M. Byler

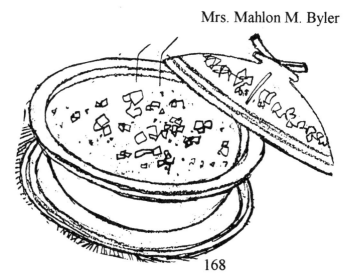

168

BARBECUED BEANS

2 cans (no. 2) pork and beans   1 c. brown sugar
1 can (no. 2) lima beans   1 c. catsup
2 medium onions   2 tbsp. mustard
3 or 4 slices bacon (cut up)   2 tbsp. vinegar

Boil brown sugar, catsup, mustard and vinegar for a few minutes. Add onion, bacon and beans. Mix together and bake at 350° for one hour or cook on top of stove, stirring occasionally.

Anna Marie Weaver

FIRE AND ICE TOMATOES

Peel and slice a couple of large tomatoes. Slice 2 onions thin. Boil the following mixture for one minute. Pour over onions and tomatoes, then refrigerate.

3/4 c. vinegar   1-1/2 tsp. salt and pepper
1-1/2 tsp. celery salt   4 tbsp. sugar
1-1/2 tsp. mustard seed   1/4 c. water

Mrs. Jake A. Byler

Vegetables and Salads

NOTES ON FAVORITE RECIPES

COCONUT SQUASH

2 c. mashed squash
1/2 c. grated coconut
2 well beaten egg yolks
1 c. fine biscuit crumbs or
  bread crumbs
1-1/2 c. milk

1 c. sugar
3 tbsp. melted butter
1-1/2 tsp. grated
  orange peel
1/2 tsp. nutmeg
3/4 tsp. salt

Meringue;
2 egg whites

2 tbsp. sugar

Mix all ingredients except those for meringue, thoroughly.
Bake slowly in a casserole until mixture thickens and is slightly
browned. Make meringue by beating egg whites until stiff and
adding 2 tbsp. sugar. Spread over squash and brown in 350°
oven for about 12 minutes.

TOMATO CASSEROLE

Slice raw, peeled tomatoes in a cake pan. On this arrange
pepper and onion rings. Season with sugar, salt and pepper.
Cover with bread crumbs, seasoned with salt, pepper and butter
as for filling. Bake in moderate oven for 1 to 1-1/2 hours.

TOMATO GRAVY

1 c. tomato juice
1/2 c. water
3 tbsp. flour
2 tbsp. sugar (optional)

1/2 tsp. salt
1/2 c. cream
2 c. milk

Place juice and water in saucepan and bring to a boil.
Meanwhile, blend the flour and salt with the cream. Add the
milk and mix well. Pour into hot juice, stirring constantly until it
boils and is thickened. May be served with bread, toast,
crackers or fried potatoes.

BAKED CARROTS

2-1/2 c. cooked, mashed carrots
1 tbsp. onion, minced
1 tsp. salt
dash of pepper

3 eggs, separated
1/2 c. bread crumbs
2 c. milk
2 tbsp. butter

Cook onions in butter until soft. Add carrots. Add beaten egg yolks, milk, celery, seasoning and bread crumbs. Beat egg whites and fold in. Place in greased baking dish and bake at 350° for 40 minutes.

LIMA BEAN CASSEROLE

1 lb. lima beans
salt and pepper
2 tbsp. onions (finely chopped)

1 c. sour cream
1 tsp. dry mustard
2 slices bacon
1/2 c. brown sugar

Soak beans overnight. Drain and cover with fresh water. Season with salt and pepper. When beans are done, drain well. Combine cooked limas with onions, brown sugar, sour cream. Put in casserole. Mix some cut up bacon in beans; put rest on top. Bake at 350° for 45 minutes.

Laura V. Troyer

AMISH WISDOM

*Success and failure
are not necessarily final.*

******

*One of the fine arts is
the fine art of living in harmony.*

ONION PATTIES
(Tastes just like onion rings!)

3/4 c. flour	2 tsp. baking powder
1 tbsp. sugar	2 tsp. salt
1 tbsp. cornmeal	3/4 c. milk
2-1/2 c. onion, finely chopped	

Mix dry ingredients together; then add milk. Batter should be fairly thick. Add onions and mix thoroughly. Drop by tablespoonfuls into 1/2 inch of oil in skillet. Flatten slightly when you turn them. Brown on both sides until crisp.

Mrs. Melvin C. Miller

POTATO SALAD

6 lg. potatoes, cooked	1 c. salad dressing
1 medium onion	2 tsp vinegar
5 boiled eggs	2 tbsp. mustard
3/4 c. sugar	2 tsp. celery seed

Dice potatoes, eggs and onions and toss together. Mix sugar, salad dressing, vinegar, mustard and celery seed into potato mixture. Blend well. Chill.

Barbara Weaver

WATERLESS COOKED PEAS

Place uncooked peas in a saucepan on very low heat, without water. Cook until tender. They'll have a much better flavor.

MASHED SWEET POTATOES

4 lg. sweet potatoes	1 c. brown sugar
1 tsp. salt	marshmallows
3/4 c. rich milk	
(1/2 cream 1/2 milk))	

Wash, peel and cook sweet potatoes. Add salt to water. Drain. Add brown sugar and milk and mash all together. Put in a casserole and cover top with marshmallows. Put in 375° oven and brown lightly.

Mrs. Andy B. A. Byler

CREAMED CELERY

1 qt. finely cut celery	1 tbsp. flour
1/2 tsp. salt	1/2 to 3/4 c. milk
1/2 c. sugar	2 tbsp. mayonnaise
2 tbsp. vinegar	

Cook celery, salt, sugar and vinegar just until tender. Use as little water as possible. Make a sauce with the flour and milk and bring to a boil. Then stir in mayonnaise or salad dressing. Mix with celery. Serve hot.

Mrs. Andy B. A. Byler

GARDEN SLAW

8 c. cabbage - shredded	1/2 c. onions - chopped
2 carrots - shredded	1 green pepper - diced
1/2 c. cold water	1 env. Knox gelatin

Pour 1/2 c. water over vegetables and set aside. Soften an envelope of Knox gelatin in cold water.

Mix together:

2/3 c. vinegar	1-1/2 tsp. salt
2/3 c. sugar	dash of pepper
2 tsp. celery seed	2/3 c. salad oil
1 envelope Knox unflavored gelatin	

Bring vinegar, sugar, celery seed, salt and pepper to a boil. Remove from heat and add gelatin and salad oil. Beat with beater. Drain vegetables and pour dressing over it and chill thoroughly. This is best if made the day before used. Keeps well in refrigerator.

Mrs. Eli E. Wengerd

TASTY GREEN BEANS

1 lb. ground beef	1 tbsp. sugar
1 qt. green beans, drained	1/2 tsp. seasoned salt
3 c. tomato juice	

Slightly brown ground beef. Pour off fat. Add all other ingredients and simmer for 20 minutes.

Mrs. Maylon M. Byler

TWENTY-FOUR-HOUR BEAN SALAD

1 15-1/2 oz. can yellow
  wax beans
1 16 oz. can green beans
1 17 oz. can kidney beans
1 can lima beans
1 c. thinly sliced onions

1/4 c. salad oil
1/2 c. vinegar
1/2 tsp. salt
3/4 c. sugar
1/4 tsp. pepper

Drain all beans; add onions. In a jar combine oil, vinegar, sugar, salt and pepper. Shake until blended. Pour over beans; let stand overnight in refrigerator.

Liz Miller

CALIFORNIA SALAD

24 marshmallows, cut up

1 lg. can pineapple
  chunks (drained and cut
  in half - save juice)

Mix above and set in cool place. Make following sauce:

2 tbsp. flour
1 c. sugar
pineapple juice

2 eggs, well beaten
1 c. whipped cream

Cook in double boiler until thick. When cool, add whipped cream. Mix with fruit mixture and serve.

Mrs. Raymond M. Miller

LIME JELLO SALAD

1/2 c. nuts	1 c. butter
2 c. flour	1/2 c. brown sugar

Mix well and press in bottom of pan and bake for 15 to 20 minutes at 375°.

Filling:

1 lg. can crushed pineapple	1 c. sugar
1 6 oz. pkg. lime Jello	1 pint whipped cream
1 8 oz. pkg. cream cheese	

Drain pineapple and put juice in a saucepan. Bring to a boil. Dissolve lime Jello in hot juice and let cool. Mix cream cheese with sugar. Blend in Jello and pineapple. Mix whipped cream with pineapple mixture. Put on top of baked crust.

Mrs. Harvey W. Byler

REFRIGERATOR COLE SLAW

1 med. head cabbage, grated	1 c. celery - chopped
1 green pepper, diced fine	1 small onion - finely chopped

Mix 1-1/2 c. sugar with	
1/2 c. white vinegar	1 tsp. celery seed
1 tsp. mustard seed	2 tsp. salt

Mix all ingredients well and refrigerate. Stays delicious for a few weeks.

Mrs. Emma Yoder

GOLDEN CARROT SALAD

1 envelope Knox unflavored gelatin
3/4 c. canned pineapple juice
1/4 c. orange juice
1 c. well drained, diced canned pineapple
1/2 c. orange sections cut in small pieces
1/2 . coarsely grated raw carrots
1/4 c. vinegar
1/4 c. sugar
1/4 tsp. salt

Mix gelatin, sugar and salt in a saucepan. Add pineapple juice. Place over low heat, stirring constantly until gelatin is dissolved. Stir in orange juice and vinegar after removing from heat. Fold in pineapple, oranges and carrots. Pour in mold and refrigerate until set.

Mrs. Ervin E. C. Miller

QUICK CHEESE SALAD

1 lb. cottage cheese
1 sm. box strawberry Jello
1 c. whipped cream
1 No. 2 can crushed pineapple

Mix all ingredients together and chill. Do not add water to Jello. Serves four.

Mrs. Jake A. Byler

PINEAPPLE SLICE SALAD

1 can Eagle Brand milk   1 lg. can pineapple slices

Boil condensed milk in a saucepan of hot water (do not open can) for 1-1/2 hour. Place pineapple slices on plate. When can of milk has cooled, open both ends of can and put out on to a small plate. Slice and put one slice on top of each pineapple slice. Top with whipped cream.

Mrs. Jake A. Byler

EGG PLATE SALAD

5 hard boiled eggs   1 c. salad dressing
6 slices fried bacon   1 tsp. vinegar
2 c. shredded cheese   3 tbsp. sugar
lettuce   2 tbsp. milk

Line plate with lettuce leaves. Slice boiled eggs. Crumble bacon over eggs and put cheese on. About 15 minutes before serving time, mix salad dressing with vinegar, sugar and milk. Mix dressing well. Drizzle over salad.

Liz Miller

HAM AND MACARONI SALAD

2 c. elbow macaroni, cooked   1 lb. cooked ham, cubed
1/2 c. mayonnaise   1/2 lb. Swiss cheese,
1/2 c. sour cream   cubed
2 to 3 tbsp. vinegar   1 small chopped onion
1 tsp. salt   1/2 c. celery, chopped

Mix and serve on lettuce leaves.

Mrs. Joe Weaver

PINEAPPLE DELIGHT

6 bananas
24 marshmallows

1 lg. can chunk pineapple, drained

Mix together and set in cool place.

Dressing:
2 tbsp. flour
1 c. sugar
1 pt. whipped cream

pineapple juice
2 eggs, well beaten

Mix dressing and cook in double boiler until thick. When cool and ready to serve, add whipped cream to fruit mixture. Some peanuts and oranges are also good added.

Mrs. Emma Weaver

TROPICAL SALAD

1 c. miniature marshmallows
1 c. orange sections, drained
1 c. pineapple tidbits, drained

1/2 c. coconut, shredded
1 c. sour cream

Mix together and place in refrigerator to chill until ready to serve.

Esther Schmucker

WATERGATE SALAD

1 pkg. pistachio instant pudding
2 oz. can crushed pineapple

1 9 oz. container Cool Whip

Mix all together and refrigerate for several hours.

Mrs. Chris Troyer

CRANBERRY SALAD

1 lb. fresh cranberries
6 oz. raspberry Jello
2 c. sugar
1 c. seeded red grapes

1 small can crushed
   pineapple
1 c. broken walnuts

Combine cranberries, sugar and 3 c. water in a large saucepan.
Bring to boil and boil until cranberries pop. Boil one minute
longer. Remove from heat and add Jello, stirring until dissolved.
Then add grapes, pineapple and nuts. Refrigerate until set.

Fannie D. Miller

CHICKEN SALAD

8 c. diced chicken
4 c. diced celery
8 eggs, hard boiled and
   cut fine

3/4 c. chopped olives
2 c. salad dressing
1 tsp. salt

Toss ingredients together. Add salad dressing. Chill and serve
on lettuce leaf.

Mrs. Owen Schmucker

MARTHA'S QUICK FRUIT SALAD

1 can fruit cocktail
1 can mandarin oranges
1 c. miniature marshmallows
2 c. whipped cream

1/2 c. nuts
8 oz. cream cheese
1/2 c. sugar

Drain fruit and add apples, marshmallows and nuts. In another
bowl, mix cream cheese and sugar until dissolved. Mix in with
fruit mixture and chill.

Betty Shrock

GARDEN SALAD

1 green pepper, chopped
1/2 c. chopped onion
8 c. shredded cabbage
2 carrots, shredded
1 pkg. unflavored gelatin
2/3 c. vinegar

2/3 c. sugar
1-1/2 tsp. salt
1/4 tsp. black pepper
2/3 c. salad oil
3/4 c. cold water

Mix cabbage, carrots, pepper and onions. Pour 1/2 c. cold water over this and chill for 1/2 hour. Soften gelatin in 1/4 c. cold water. Set aside. Mix sugar, vinegar, black pepper and bring to boil. Remove from heat and stir in oil. Drain vegetables, pour on dressing, mix lightly. Store in refrigerator.

Kathryn Byler

PEA SALAD

1/2 head shredded lettuce
1 lb. bacon (crisply fried)
2 pkg. frozen peas (thawed)
6 hard boiled eggs (chopped)

1/2 med. onion, minced
1 pt. salad dressing
1 c. shredded Swiss
cheese

Mix peas, bacon pieces, eggs, onion and salad dressing. Spread on top of lettuce and sprinkle with cheese. Serve chilled.

Mrs. John E. Miller

HOT DANDELION GREENS

Wash and cut to one inch young dandelion plant. Use plant before any blossoms arrive. To one quart of greens add two hard cooked eggs, cooled and coarsely chopped. Make dressing as follows:

2 tbsp. margarine	2 tbsp. vinegar
3 tbsp. flour	salt and pepper to taste
1 c. milk	

Place margarine in heavy skillet. Add flour and brown both slightly. Add one cup milk or more to make thick gravy. Add vinegar, salt and pepper to taste. Toss through salad and serve immediately.

NOODLES

6 egg yolks	3 c. flour (approx.)
6 tbsp. water	pinch of salt

Beat egg yolks and water a few minutes. Add flour to make dough. Make stiff, just so it can be worked. Divide into four balls, roll very thin. Lay separately on a cloth until they won't stick together. Then lay on top of each other, roll all together and cut as desired. A meat slicer works very well for slicing. Makes one pound.

Mrs. Elmer Hostetler

RIBBON SALAD

First Layer:

2 pkg. lime Jello   4 c. hot water

Mix above and put in oblong dish and let chill until firm.

Second Layer:

1 pkg. lime Jello   1 c. hot water
1 pkg.sm. marshmallows   1 lg. pkg. cream cheese
1 No. 2 can crshed. pineapple 1 c. whipping cream

Mix lime Jello with very hot water. Dissolve cream cheese and marshmallows in hot Jello. Add pineapple. Chill, and when Jello is starting to set, add whipping cream. Pour on set lime Jello.

Third Layer:

2 pkg. cherry Jello   4 c. hot water

Mix above. When starting to set, pour on second layer. Chill to firm. Can be cut in squares and placed on lettuce leaf.

Lucie Byler

AMISH DRESSING

1 loaf bread, diced and   1/2 tsp. sage
  toasted   1/2 tsp. thyme
4 eggs   3/4 c. diced potatoes
1 med. onion - chopped   2 c. diced chicken
  fine   1/2 c. diced and cooked
1/2 tsp. salt   carrots
1/8 tsp. pepper   3 stalks celery, minced
(continued)

183

Put eggs in bowl and beat. Add salt, pepper, sage, and thyme. Mix. Add 2 cups milk, onions, celery, potatoes, diced chicken and carrots. Add bread crumbs and enough milk to moisten well. Substitute 1 c. chicken broth instead of milk if desired. Bake in well-greased in 9 " casserole at 350°

TURKEY DRESSING

1-1/2 loaf bread	1 stick margarine
4 eggs	1 c. milk
1/3 c. celery flakes	1/4 tsp. sage
3/4 c. cooked potatoes, diced	2 c. chicken broth
	1 tbsp. parsley flakes
1 tsp. salt	1/2 tsp. pepper

Cut bread into cubes and brown in a pan with butter. Put a stick of margarine over hot, cooked potatoes or in hot broth to melt. Then add beaten eggs and rest of ingredients. Add bread cubes last and cool before stuffing turkey.

GRANOLA CEREAL

4 c. old fashioned rolled oats	1/2 c. vegetable oil
	2/3 c. honey
4 oz. coconut	1-1/2 tsp. cinnamon
1/2 c. wheat germ	1/2 c. sesame seeds
1/2 tsp. nutmeg	1 c. chopped nuts
2 tbsp. vanilla	
1 c. raisins	

Mix all ingredients together. Mix honey, oil, vanilla together. Pour over dry ingredients, blend well. Divide in 2 parts. Sprinkle evenly on two cookie sheets and bake 18 minutes at 300°. Stir occasionally and watch carefully as it burns quickly around edges. Cool. Add 1 c. raisins or dates. Store in tightly covered container. Serve with cold milk.

Mrs. Ervin E. C. Miller

NOTES ON FAVORITE RECIPES

Miscellaneous

NOTES ON FAVORITE RECIPES

HOMEMADE GRAPENUTS

14 c. graham flour
4 c. brown sugar
8 c. sour milk

1 tsp. salt
4 tsp. soda

Mix ingredients thoroughly. Spread dough 1/4 in. thick on flat greased cookie sheet and bake at 400° for 15 to 25 min. When done crumble them and brown in oven until crisp. Serve with sugar and milk. Makes 4 batches.

PARTY MIX

1 box Cherrios
1 box Rice Chex
2 bags pretzels
2 cans mixed nuts
1 tbsp. garlic salt

3/4 c. margarine -
  melted
1 tbsp. celery salt
1 tbsp. onion salt

Mix cereals, pretzels and nuts together. Mix salts into melted margarine and pour over dry ingredients. Spread into large roaster or pan, cover with foil. Bake at 200° for 1 hour. Uncover and bake 1 hour, stirring every 15 minutes. Cool and store in tight containers.

Mrs. Allen Detweiler

PIZZA

Dough:
3/4 c. water
1 pkg. yeast

2-1/2 c. biscuit mix

Dissolve yeast in warm water. Add biscuit mix. Beat vigorously. Turn onto surface dusted with biscuit mix. Knead about 20 times. Preheat oven to 425°
(continued)

Sauce:

1/2 c. chopped onion	1-1/2 tsp. sugar
1 clove garlic	1/2 tsp. chili powder
1 6 oz. can tomato paste	1/4 tsp. pepper
1 8 oz. can tomato sauce	2 tsp. salt
1 c. grated mozzarella cheese	

Fry onions and garlic slowly in hot fat until tender. Stir in tomato sauce, paste and seasoning. Heat together. Sprinkle grated mozzarella cheese on top. Top with either pepperoni, sausage, crumbled fried bacon, green peppers or mushrooms. Makes two 12" pizzas.

Alma Miller

PIZZA SAUCE

3 lbs. onions	1/2 bushel tomatoes
4-6 hot peppers	3 garlic cloves
1 pt. vegetable oil	

Cook above until soft, then put through sieve. Add vegetable oil and then add:

8 small cans tomato paste	1 tbsp. oregano leaves
1 tbsp. basil	1-1/2 c. sugar
1/2 c. salt	

Simmer 2-5 hours. (I simmer mine longer as I like it thick.) Stir every once in a while. Pack in jars and seal. Can be used for pizza, sloppy joes or spaghetti.

Alma Miller

SPAGHETTI SAUCE

1/2 bushel tomatoes
6 green peppers
10 onions
3 lb. hamburger

pinch of red pepper
1 can of cheese
1-1/2 c. sugar
salt and pepper to taste

Cook tomatoes, peppers and onions until they are juicy. Add hamburger, cheese, sugar, salt and pepper. Cook for four hours over low heat. Makes 12-15 quarts.

Mrs. Ervin E. Yoder

PIZZA ON A BUN

1 sm. can pimentos
1 10 oz. pkg. cracker
  barrel cheese
8 strips bacon, fried

2 green peppers
4 hard boiled eggs
hamburger buns
1 bottle chili sauce

Grind pimentos, cheese, bacon, peppers and eggs. Mix with chili sauce and spread on hamburger buns. Put under broiler or in oven for 8 to 10 minutes until cheese melts and browns lightly.

Liz Miller

CATSUP

1 peck tomatoes
4 onions
3 red peppers
1 c. vinegar
3 c. sugar
(continued)

1 tsp. mixed pickle
  spices
1 tbsp. salt
1 tbsp. turmeric
1/4 tsp. pepper

187

Skin tomatoes and cook until soft. Put through a sieve. Add remaining ingredients and boil until thick. Put in sterile jars or bottles with tight lids.

Mrs. Andy B. A. Byler

TOSSED SALAD DRESSING

1 tbsp. grated onion
1/2 c. sugar
1/2 c. vegetable oil
1/4 c. vinegar

1 tsp. salt
1/2 tsp. paprika
1 tbsp. lemon juice
1/3 c. catsup

Mix all ingredients. Store in refrigerator. Makes 1-1/2 cups.

Mrs. Harvey W. Byler

QUICK SALAD DRESSING

3 parts oil
1 part vinegar

salt
pepper

Shake well and pour over fresh salad greens.

Mrs. Andy B. A. Byler

MOCK SHAKE AND BAKE

1 c. flour
2 tsp. paprika
dash of pepper

1 tsp. baking powder
1/2 tsp. salt

Mix all ingredients together and use as you would Shake and Bake on chicken and pork chops.

Mrs. Dan J. M. Miller

HERB SAUCE FOR GREEN BEANS

2 tbsp. oil
1 c. tomatoes
1 tsp. marjoram
1/2 tsp. seasoned salt
1 tbsp. celery flakes

1/2 tsp. garlic powder
1 tbsp. onion flakes
1 tbsp. green pepper
  flakes

Combine ingredients in sauce pan. Simmer for 5 minutes, pour over cooked green beans. Makes enough for 4 cups cooked beans.

Mrs. Emma Byler

REFRIGERATOR PICKLES

6 c. sliced cukes
2 onions (sliced)
1 c. vinegar
2 c. sugar

1 tbsp. pickling or
  regular salt
1 tbsp. celery seed

Bring vinegar, salt, celery seed and sugar to boil. Cook, pour over cukes and onions. Refrigerate.

Mrs. Dan J. M. Miller

UNDER THE SEA SALAD

2 pkgs. lime Jell-O - make
  as directed on box
1 pint whipping cream

1 can crushed pineapple
1/2 lb. miniature
  marshmallows

Whip cream and blend in softened cream cheese. Fold in pineapple and marshmallows. Spread in large loaf pan and cover mixture with warm Jell-O. Jell-O will sink to bottom of pan. Cut in squares when firm and serve on a lettuce leaf.

Mrs. Allen Mullet

BUTTERSCOTCH SAUCE FOR ICE CREAM

1 lb. brown sugar
1/2 c. butter
1/2 pint cream

1/2 tsp. vanilla
pinch of salt

Cook for 1 hour in double boiler over slow heat, stirring occasionally. Remove from heat. Add vanilla last and mix.

Mrs. Andy B. A. Byler

STRAWBERRY TOPPING

1 qt. mashed strawberries
1 qt. sugar

1 pkg. Sure-Jel
1 c. boiling water

Stir sugar and strawberries together until sugar is melted. Bring Sure-Jel and water to a boil and immediately stir into berries. Stir for 5 minutes. Put in containers and freeze.

Mrs. Andy B. A. Byler

HOT CHOCOLATE MIX

1 c. powdered sugar
6 oz. can Cremora

2 lbs. box quick chocolate
8 qt. box powdered milk

Mix 3 tsp. to 1 c. hot water.

Mrs. William W. Hochstetler

SUNSET PUNCH

1 c. Tang   1 28 oz. bottle ginger
1-1/2 c. pineapple juice   ale or club soda

Stir until Tang is completely dissolved. Pour over ice. Makes 12-14 servings,

Mrs. Emma Byler

ROOT BEER

2 c. sugar   4 tsp. root beer extract
1 tsp. yeast

Dissolve yeast in small amount of warm water. Melt sugar in small amount of hot water. Pour into gallon jug. Add root beer extract to yeast mixture. Fill jug with lukewarm water. Sit jug in sun for 3 hours. Refrigerate and serve cold.

Ella Byler

RASPBERRY PUNCH

1 can Hawaiian Punch - red   1 qt. orange soda
2 qts. 7-UP   1 qt. raspberry sherbet

Mix red punch, orange soda and 7-UP in punch bowl. Spoon sherbet on top of punch. Ice cubes can be made in advance, using some of the punch mixture to drop into the punch at the last minute with the sherbet.

ICE TEA SYRUP

2-1/2 c. sugar
4 c. boiling water

1 c. loose tea

Let water and tea leaves steep for 15 minutes; strain. Add sugar. Boil for 10 minutes. This will make 1 qt. of syrup. Put 1 tbsp. syrup in a glass, then fill with water and ice. This should make 1 gallon of iced tea.

Mrs. Mahlon M. Byler

GOLD STRIKE PUNCH

6 eggs, slightly beaten
4-1/2 c. chilled cranberry
 juice
1-1/2 c. chilled orange
 juice

2/3 c. honey or sugar
1/3 c. lemon juice
orange & lemon slices

Combine first 5 ingredients, beat well until thoroughly blended. Pour into punch bowl. Garnish with orange and lemon slices if desired. Make 16 punch cup servings.

Mrs. Mahlon M. Byler

BREAKFAST NOG FOR ONE

1 egg
1 c. milk
1 tbsp. honey of sugar

1 tsp. vanilla
dash of nutmeg and
 cinnamon (optional)

Blend together and chill.

Mrs. Mahlon M. Byler

EYE OPENER

1 egg   1/4 tsp. salt
1 c. tomato juice   dash of tabasco sauce

Combine all ingredients, beat with fork just until dissolved. Pour into tall glass.

Mrs. Mahlon M. Byler

STRAWBERRY PUNCH

3 qts. strawberries   2 lg. cans frozen
6 qts. ginger ale   Minute Maid lemonade
1 fifth Black Velvet Whiskey

If using fresh strawberries, add sugar to taste. Blend together and chill.

Mrs. Allen Detweiler

GREEN PUNCH

1 qt. 50/50 pop   1 qt. pineapple juice
2 qts. ginger ale   2 qt. lime sherbet

Mix above ingredients in large punch bowl. Add sherbet. Stir lightly.

Kathryn Hostetler

RED BEET JELLY

6 c. beet juice
1/2 c. lemon juice
2 Sure-Jel

8 c. sugar
2 sm. pkgs. raspberry
Jell-O

Mix all ingredients together. Boil for 5-10 minutes. Pour into sterile jars and seal. Tastes like raspberry jelly.

Mrs. Urie M. Byler

RHUBARB PRESERVES

4 c. rhubarb, cut up
4 c. sugar

1 sm. can crushed pineapple
1 sm. box strawberry Jell-O

Wash and prepare rhubarb, add sugar. Let stand 2-1/2 hours, mixing occasionally. Bring to boil and boil for ten minutes. Add pineapple. Boil again for 7 minutes. Remove from heat and add Jell-O. Seal in sterile jars.

Mrs. Raymond M. Miller

SWEETENED CONDENSED MILK

1 c. dry milk
1/2 c. boiling water

2/3 c. sugar
3 tbsp. butter, melted

Beat all ingredients with a beater or process in a blender until thickened and smooth. Make 1-1/4 cup or equivalent of 14 oz. can of milk. Keep refrigerated.

Katherine M. Byler

HOUSEHOLD HINTS

Dry green celery or parsley leaves until crumbly. Store in covered jars to use as seasoning in soups.

After rice has been cooked and drained, place a slice of dry bread on top of the rice and cover. The bread will absorb the moisture and the rice will be dry and fluffy.

Before melting chocolate, rub the inside of the pan it is to be melted in with butter. The chocolate will not stick to the pan.

When washing pans and baking dishes to which food has adhered during cooking, turn the pan upside down in steaming sudsy water. Food will loosen in a very short time.

When cookie dough is soft and difficult to handle place it between pieces of waxed paper that have been floured. Roll to desired thickness, remove top paper and cut cookies.

Singe chicken or other foul by holding over burner of gas stove.

To get fruit juices that are difficult to gel, such as peach juice, add 1-1/2 tsp. plain gelatin to each cup of juice. Soften gelatin in 3 teaspoons juice and add to remaining hot juice. Add 1 teaspoon lemon juice to each quart of fruit juice.

Before discarding the empty catsup bottle, pour some vinegar into the bottle and use in making French dressing.

Pour melted paraffin on the cut end of cheese or dried beef to keep them from molding or drying out.

To improve the flavor of green string beans, place 1 or 2 small onions in kettle before adding beans.

When baking whole fish, wrap in well-oiled cheesecloth. When fish is done, it can be lifted from baking pan without falling to pieces. To remove cloth slip a spatula under fish and slide cloth out after fish is on platter.

Stick 2 or 3 pieces of macaroni in the center of a double crust pie. When juice bubbles up these prevent the pie from running over.

To prevent onions from burning your eyes hold them under water when peeling or slicing them.

Contributed by Mrs. Jonas V. Miller

Whitener for cottons and some manmade fabrics: Pour one gallon hot water into plastic bucket. Add one cup Cascade or other electric dishwasher soap and one cup of Clorox or household bleach. Stir well, dip garment in this mixture and soak from 1/4 to 1/2 hour. Wash as usual. Put 1/2 cup vinegar in rinse water.

Contributed by Mrs. Emma Byler

FERTILIZER FOR HOUSE PLANTS
Do Not Eat!

1 tsp. salt peter   1 tsp. household ammonia
1 tsp. baking powder   1 gallon water
1 tsp. epsom salts

Mix and stir well. Use small amount on house plants once a month.

Contributed by Mrs. Emma Byler

Home Remedies

NOTES ON FAVORITE RECIPES

HOME REMEDIES

We wish to stress the importance of contacting your physician in the event of illness and discussing these home remedies with him. His diagnosis is important. Be sure to get his approval before trying any of the following. The following remedies were contributed by Mrs. Emma A. Byler:

Blood Cleaner

Anything you use as a blood cleaner will thin your blood and if high blood pressure is a patient's problem, it should not be used, as it will raise the blood pressure more.

sassafras tea
red clover blossom tea) use only 1 cup per day
strawberry leaf tea   )
dandelion root or leaf tea

Brew any of these teas as you would Chinese tea and drink one cup a day for three weeks.

Liver Ailments - Eat rhubarb sauce and it will get rid of mucus and acid of the liver.

Rosemary Herb was used for many ills, for example failing memory or as heart tonic. Is also used to flavor beef roast, chicken, tomato soup.

Sage - Use teas as remedy for flu, sore throats, and nervous headaches. Makes men wise and improves their memory faculties (hence, sage plant). Also use for flavoring for chicken stuffing and sausages.

(continued)

197

Female Problems/Painful Periods - Use tea made of red raspberry leaves - 1 tsp. dry crumbled leaves to 1 cup boiling water. Sweeten with honey and drink hot. Use no more than 2 cups in 24 hours.

Pneumonia - Drink bone set tea, hot, twice a day.
Drink lots of fluids:

3 c. hot water   )
1/2 c. lemon juice) drink hot, all in one day
honey to sweeten   )

Aids for High Blood Pressure - Drink any of the following teas, no more than one cup daily. All may be mixed and use 1 tsp. to one cup of boiling water.

1. Chamomile (flower head)
2. Blue Vervain (whole plant)
3. Comfrey (leaves and root)
4. Catnip (whole plant)

Cancer and Tumor Remedy - 2 cups red clover blossom, 1 tablespoon ginger root (cut fine). Add one quart after and boil down to one pint. Drain and let liquid cool. Add 1 tsp. of blood root liquid that you can buy in drugstore. Add one pint of good whiskey. Mix and put in bottle and keep in cool place. Take one teaspoon three times a day until all is used up.

This is also a good tonic to use once a year or if run down.

Red clover blossom tea is a good tonic in itself and will clear up many infections.

(continued)

Drawing Salve for Blood Poison:

1/4 lb. beeswax
1/4 lb. rosin
1-1/4 lb. sheep tallow
2 oz. gum camphor
3 oz. homemade soft soap

Melt first four ingredients together in old pan. When hot, add soap a little at a time and boil slowly until well mixed. Pour into small jars while still warm. (Small baby food jars are fine). For drawing out pain and poison, make a thick plaster and apply. Leave bandage on eight hours for healing. Apply only a thin coat of the bandage.

To heal (1) Broken Bones; (2) Weak Lungs; (3) Any Infection of the Body; (4) Rundown Conditions:

Drink Bone Set Tea, Comfrey Tea made with leaf and dried root of the plant. Every home should have a Comfrey plant by the back door - easy to raise and ornamental as well. Roots of herbs should be stewed a minute or two to get all the strength; leaves should be brewed as with any tea.

Boneset Tea - Mix 4 tsp. leaves and flower head (crumbled), to one quart boiling water. (Honey may be added to sweeten.) Strain. This will keep in ice box for several days. Drink hot or cold.

Tobacco Salve for Cough and Congestion
2 lbs. lard
1 lb. Cutty pipe tobacco (fine) (We use "Bull Durham")
1/2 lb. seeded raisins

Put all in pan and cook 1/2 hour on slow heat, stirring all the time. Strain and put in 1/2 pint jars. Use as plaster on chest.

Nerve Medicine without Drugs:

(1) Blue Vervain Herb: Brew 2 tsp. crushed leaves and flower head in 2 cups boiling water. Drink one cup warm before retiring and one cup next day. Sweeten with honey.

(2) Catnip and chamomile tea will serve equally well. Use blossom only. With catnip, use any of the plant.

Sore Throat:

(1) Take off your dirty socks at bedtime and tie or pin around the throat. This is an old remedy and somehow it seems to help.

(2) Gargle with blood root tea, made with a 2 inch piece of root. Cut fine and brew in one cup hot water. Let simmer a minute. Gargle as hot as one can stand.

Oncoming Cold:

(1) Gargle with any hot liquid. Hot water will do.

(2) Gargle with salt water.

(3) Gargle with hot lemon tea.

The hot liquid will kill germs before they leave your throat for the lungs, etc.

Asthma Congestion - Add 1 oz. of the inner bark or pith of the wild cherry tree to one quart of water and boil down to one pint. Add 1 cup of honey and 1/3 c. of horehound candy (melted). Mix well and take 1 tbsp. as needed.

Lung Fever Salve: We have cases where the doctor gave up all hope of recovery from pneumonia. This plaster was used on the chest and rib cage and on the back and the fever broke and the patient got well. Our druggist here in Middlefield has this all made up ready to heat.

4 drams balsam peru
4 drams oil of turpentine
4 drams oil of cedar
6 oz. white rosin
4 oz. gum camphor
12 oz. hog lard

Mix all ingredients in old kettle or tin can. Heat until all is melted, stir with clean stick. Strain through screen sieve and put in 1/2 pint jars.

To use plaster: Spread on flannel warm enough to make it just as warm as patient can stand it. Cover chest and back with plasters. Cover plasters with warm dry cloths. This will draw out the infections and will cause the patient to seat. Be very careful not to let patient chill. Also use as rub for chest colds.

Burns - An aloe vera plant is a very good first aid for burns and scalds. Break off leaf - the slippery ooze will seal off air from burn and will stop the pain in a few minutes. Severe or deep burns need the care of a physician.

Leave burns uncovered whenever possible. This hastens healing.

A paste made of unsalted lard and flour will also aid in taking the pain from burns.

Diarrhea - Drink juice of canned blackberry and/or blueberries.

The leaves of the shrub of blueberries are made into a tea. Drink a cup several times a day for same ailment. 2 tsp. dried leaves plus 1 pint boiling water.

Blueberry leaves are a blood purifier. Brew tea and drink war.

Also, the blossoms of the elder bush brewed is a good tonic - 1 tsp. flowers to 1 cup boiling water.

Dropsy and Kidney Trouble

Boil navy beans for 20 minutes. Drain off water and have patient drink 1/2 cup several times a day.

For Dropsy - the root of the elderberry bush is dried and then cut in fine pieces, stewed a few minutes in a pint of water. Use the whole pint in one day.

For kidney problems - Brew tea of ground ivy, 1 tsp. to cup of boiling water. Drink one cup per day.

All the roots and bark may be purchased at Indiana Botanic Gardens, PO Box 5, Hammond, Indiana 46325. (Free booklet available through above.)

TABLE OF EQUIVALENT MEASURES

1 stick (1/4 lb.) butter or margarine - 1/2 cup

1 square chocolate - 3 tablespoons cocoa

2 large eggs = 3 small eggs

1 cup macaroni = 2-1/2 cups cooked

1 cup buttermilk = 1 or 2 tablespoons vinegar with sweet milk to fill cup (let stand 5 minutes)

1 tablespoon quick-cooking tapioca = 1 tablespoon cornstarch or 1-1/2 tablespoons flour

1 package active dry yeast = 1 tablespoon

1 package plain gelatin = 1 tablespoon

1 lb. granulated sugar = 2 cups

1 lb. brown sugar = 2-1/2 cups (packed)

1 lb. confectioner's sugar = 4 to 4-1/2 cups (sifted)

1 lb. all-purpose flour = 4 cups

1 lb. butter = 2 cups

Contributed by Mrs. Jonas V. Miller

NOTES ON FAVORITE RECIPES

INDEX

BREADS AND ROLLS

BREADS AND ROLLS

CAKES, PIES & PUDDINGS

CAKES, PIES & PUDDINGS

CAKES, PIES & PUDDINGS

CAKES, PIES & PUDDINGS

CAKES, PIES & PUDDINGS

COOKIES & CANDY

COOKIES & CANDY

COOKIES & CANDY

CASSEROLES, MEATS & SOUPS

CASSEROLES, MEATS & SOUPS

CASSEROLES, MEATS & SOUPS

CASSEROLES, MEATS & SOUPS

MISCELLANEOUS

MISCELLANEOUS

ORDER FORM

The Amish Way Cookbook.............................$ 12.95
Wonderful authentic Amish recipes. Featured
in the magazine section of the Plain Dealer

The Amish Recipe Sampler..............................$ 4.95
65 delicious recipes with a charming sampler
cover and quaint sayings throughout.

Katie's Dream Storybook...................................$ 5.95
The story of a little Amish girl and her family.
A charming story with Amish customs throughout.

An Amish Potpourri Cookbook.........................$ 12.95
Over 300 great recipes plus Amish poems,
sayings and essays written by Amish folks.

Plain and Fancy Amish Cookie Recipes...............$ 6.95
100 delicious cookie recipes. 20 luscious
candy recipes. Cookies of every description.

Quantity	Title	Price each	Total
------------	------------------------	------------------	------------------
------------	------------------------	------------------	------------------
------------	------------------------	------------------	------------------

Your name_____
Address_____
Please include $1.50 postage for first book ordered. Add $.75 for
each additional book. Send check or money order to:

Jupiter Press   Phone: (216) 247-3616
77 So. Franklin St. Fax: (216) 247-5431
Chagrin Falls, OH 44022